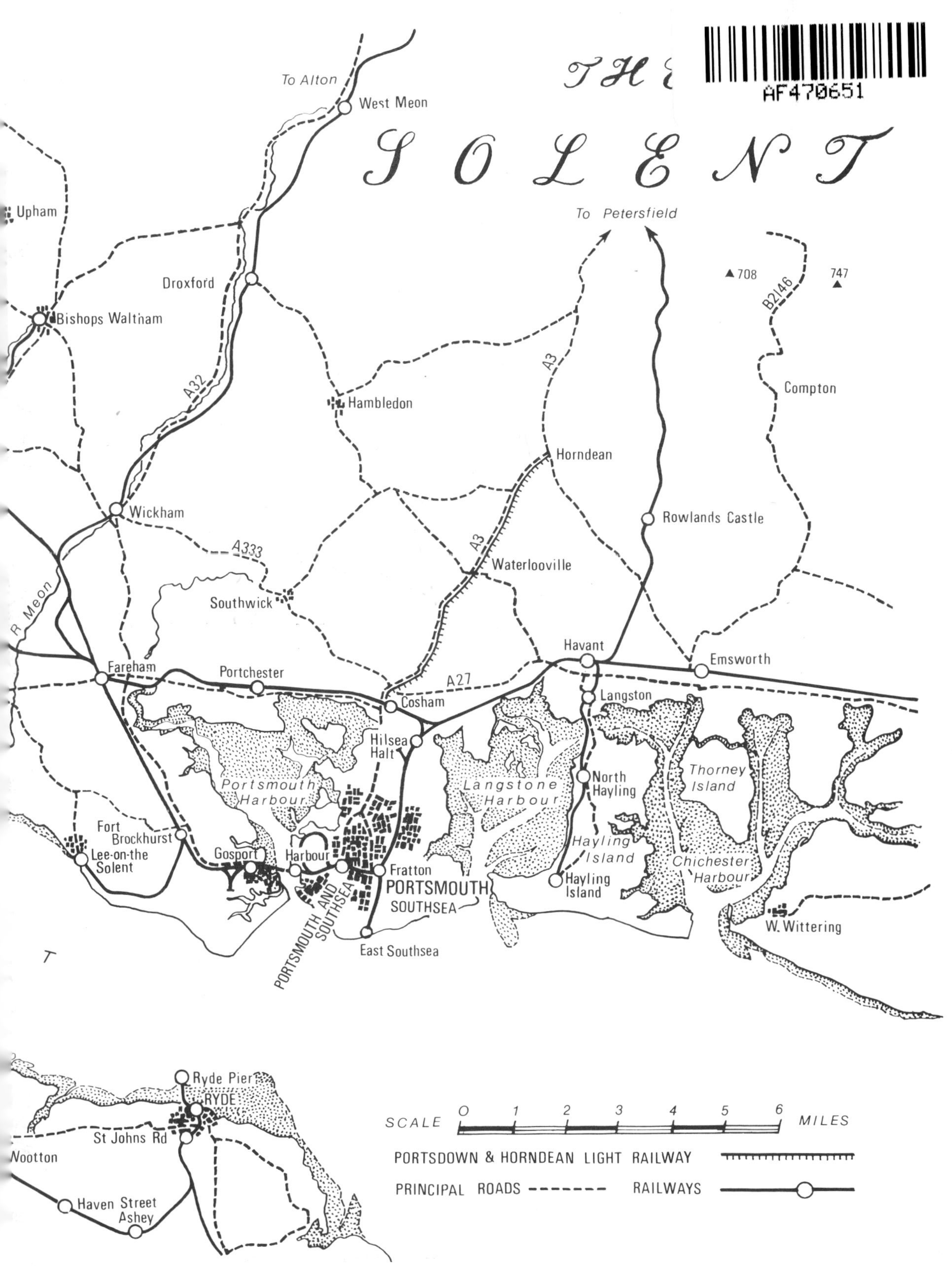
THE
SOLENT
AF470651
To Alton
West Meon
To Petersfield
Upham
708
747
Droxford
B2146
Bishops Waltham
Compton
A32
Hambledon
Horndean
Wickham
A333
Rowlands Castle
A3
Southwick
Waterlooville
A3
R Meon
Havant
Emsworth
Fareham
Portchester
A27
Langston
Cosham
Hilsea
Halt
Portsmouth
Harbour
Langstone
Harbour
Thorney
Island
North
Hayling
Fort
Brockhurst
Lee-on-the
Solent
Gosport
Harbour
Hayling
Island
Chichester
Harbour
PORTSMOUTH AND SOUTHSEA
Fratton
PORTSMOUTH
SOUTHSEA
Hayling
Island
T
East Southsea
W. Wittering
Ryde Pier
RYDE
St Johns Rd
Nootton
Haven Street
Ashey
SCALE   0   1   2   3   4   5   6   MILES
PORTSDOWN & HORNDEAN LIGHT RAILWAY
PRINCIPAL ROADS   RAILWAYS

Joyce

Recalling many years of
club activities and
ViTA membership.

Kind Regards,

David

10th October 1981.

Roads, Rails & Ferries of the Solent Area 1919-1969

As the fireman waits to collect the train-staff from the signalman at Portsmouth High Level, E1 0–6–0T No 32139 is eased for the sharp curve away from platform 6 on to the Dockyard branch on 26 March 1956. /*Author*

Roads, Rails & Ferries of the Solent Area 1919~1969

D. Fereday Glenn

IAN ALLAN LTD

First published 1980

ISBN 0 7110 1016 1

All rights reserved. No part of this book may be reproduced or transmitted in any form or by any means, electronic or mechanical, including photo-copying, recording or by any information storage and retrieval system, without permission from the Publisher in writing.

Design by Anthony Wirkus

© D. Fereday Glenn, 1980

Published by Ian Allan Ltd, Shepperton, Surrey, and printed by Ian Allan Printing Ltd at their works at Coombelands in Runnymede, England.

Title page: Typical of the Hants & Sussex coach fleet in 1950, No 201 (GOT 183) illustrates the attractive lines of a Leyland Tiger PS1 fitted with Duple coachwork for excursions and private hire duties.
/The News, Portsmouth

Right: While male bus crews joined the armed forces during the war, many women were trained as drivers and conductresses to keep the vehicles moving. New recruits find their way about on Portsmouth Corporation Leyland No 128 at Eastney.
/The News, Portsmouth

Contents

Introduction

In a world crippled with inflation and violence, many folk may be forgiven for wishing they had been born into an earlier age. An age when man was more concerned with inventing and building up, when more respect was paid to person and property, when instant media did not bring alternate doom and gloom to sully a more contented way of life. But though we may hanker after some bygone era, steeped in folklore and chivalry, we should remember that the pleasures of transport – essentially the core of this book – were being hammered out during the Industrial Revolution and the reign of Queen Victoria, a time not noted for home comforts if one was poor, as Dickens reminds us! In a word, nostalgia has a habit of cloaking the past with a sort of saintly aura that it did not really possess, for there have always been problems and disputes, dangers and difficulties from time immemorial. As John Milton said, 'The mind is its own place and of itself can make a hell of Heaven, or a heaven of Hell'; people have always tended to believe what they want to believe and the folklore of transport is no exception. Those of us who have been fortunate enough to have lived even part of our lives during the steam age of our railways are blessed indeed, but who can deny that the comfort and speed of today's Inter-City 125 is a truly great achievement in the best traditions of Stephenson or Brunel? If it had not been for the massive slaughter of coal-burning locomotives during the Beeching period – and their consequent piling up pending scrap in Woodhams' yard at Barry – many museum centres and preserved lines would have little to show of our past achievements. Among the developed nations of the world, this country has a very keen sense of its own history – an appreciation of which is available to all, in a way that our forbears would never have believed possible. We are the heirs of a most evocative period of transport development – certainly the most productive – since the creation of the wheel itself.

Going back several generations, my family has been much involved with the development of transport around the Solent. The area itself has been in the forefront of Britain's history at least since Roman times with plenty of evidence still visible to illustrate two thousand years' expansion of roads, fortresses and dockyards. Without doubt, the sea's double tidal-flow has played a part in this and it is significant that a number of important rivers and streams have their outflow along the coastline bounded by Lymington on the west and Fishbourne on the east – for the purpose of this book considered to be the seaward limitations of the 'Solent Area'. Because many excellent, scholarly works have been written dealing with the full history of particular aspects of its transport, I have tried to bring together most of the strands as they were about the time of World War I; to observe their rise and fall, the very pulse of transport's development within the Solent, through the 1920s and 1930s and World War II, through peace leading to the 1950s and a natural point of conclusion at the end of the 1960s – a full half century picture of mostly road and rail in an area encompassing both West Sussex and the New Forest. Fifty years in which the spirit of change fairly whistled through . . .

I was born only a matter of weeks after Portsmouth's last tram had rolled into the depot so that my appreciation of, and apprenticeship in, a love of transport began in the midst of strife during World War II. This book falls neatly into two parts: the first dealing with 20 years of peace between the wars and the early stages of the second conflict, followed by the climax of the war and its succeeding two decades of peace. The former I have gleaned from my elders' conversation and a number of historical sources; the latter is largely within my own experience. Like my father, I was born in Portsmouth; my mother spent her early years in Southampton. Throughout the war and for three years afterwards we lived at Hilsea, on the outskirts of Portsmouth as it was at that time. During 1948 we moved to a village on the fringe of Fareham, where the family still live, which was to prove an ideal mid-point from which to observe and experience changes at first hand throughout the Solent. Despite being 'out-stationed' at a boarding school until 1955, I was able to follow events from 20 miles inland before returning to Portsmouth as an articled clerk, with daily commuting from Fareham. My preferences were already emerging during this period, when I was most reliant upon public transport. Soon, however, I was to become more independent: on my twenty-first birthday I inherited a modest sum that enabled me to finance the purchase of a small Lambretta scooter, with which my horizons were enlarged to include such luxuries as a holiday in Scotland and summer weekends in the West Country.

After a couple of years on two wheels, culminating in a spill on Glasgow's greasy tram tracks following a thunderstorm, it seemed sensible to transfer my allegiance to four wheels in the shape of a virtuous black Austin Ruby saloon. While 40,000 miles astride a scooter was no bad effort, the aged

Right: Grandfather. John Fereday Glenn, engineer and manager, at the controls of Car No 5 (built by British Electric Car Company Ltd) on the slopes of Portsdown Hill in 1906./*D. Fereday Glenn collection*

Austin Seven achieved a further 54,000 miles on top of the 100,000 covered before my period of ownership began in 1960! Readers may be tempted to conclude that many of my studies were of matters more to do with transport than the law . . . Being advised to take up some pursuit nearer my heart, I became a motor car salesman and graduated (to modern vehicles) at last. Subsequently, first as a senior salesman at Tunbridge Wells and then as Sales Manager at Godalming, it was possible to drive cars with some particular appeal – Triumphs, Rileys and Daimlers to name but a few. With steam traction dead or dying upon British Railways in 1967, along with many fellow transport enthusiasts I yearned for something absorbing to 'take up the slack' after nearly 20 years' involvement with trains. The answer when it came was singularly obvious – to buy an omnibus!

After first travelling regularly by bus to school, I found myself literally in the driving seat of one. It took five and twenty years for the wheel to come full circle, which involved learning a wholly-new technique of driving and an added dimension to my appreciation of transport. Not to put too fine a point upon it, there was an awful lot to learn to achieve satisfaction in the handling of an eight ton monster; thwarted by non-synchromesh gears and with a steering wheel that could have doubled as a chest expander, slipping a thirty-footer through Godalming's proverbially narrow streets was a lot more demanding than one cared to admit. The acid test was to take it on an Easter trip to Devon, 500 miles behind the wheel. Perhaps the most amusing memory of that first exploit is of resting in a lay-by after surmounting a one in eight out of Moretonhampstead and watching no less than 42 cars emerge thankfully from the black pall that hung like a smokescreen over the lush green landscape, to proceed at a less inhibited pace along the B3212 towards Exeter! More recently, experiences with driving Gardner-engined double-deckers have reminded me of handling a fairground dodgem car – the time-honoured method seems to be to push the accelerator to the floor and let the governor do the rest! I think it is true to say that active preservation of an old bus – designed and built with finesse – is for me the closest one can get to true transport-rapture after Beeching. Having almost 100% mobility to visit rail centres, museums, tramway enclaves or even travel abroad, a preserved bus goes a long way to unifying all one's transport interests 'under one cab', so to speak.

In preparing this volume I am conscious how much assistance I have received from fellow enthusiasts and transport people. The bulk of the photographs and subject matter falls within the period 1919-1969 and I hope that some of each will prove to be new and stimulating to those more versed in transport history than I. In particular, I should like to thank *Portsmouth & Sunderland Newspapers Ltd* and *Southern Newspapers Ltd* for access to their archives, both Portsmouth and Southampton City Museums, the Portsmouth City Archivist, Science Museum, National Railway Museum, Norman Hamshere, Denis Clarke, E. C. Griffith, Tim Jackman, Ron Brown, Peter Tame and Gosport Museum for the use of certain photographs; Margaret Lovell for patiently assisting with corrections to the manuscript; and Norman Facy for his unfailing perfection in making prints from dozens of negatives. The whole task has been a journey of discovery through a period before my time to one I thought I knew moderately well! The Solent area has been 'home' for much of my life – I hope it will be as fascinating to you as it has been for me, in the pages of this book.

Epoch I

1919~1929, The End of the Beginning

1
Return of the Heroes

My mother told me the tale of how, when she was a little girl, she had been taken from her home at Millbrook into Southampton to see the troops come back from the Great War. One can picture the streets – much narrower than they are today – thronged with people, standing on railings, clinging to gaslamps, anything to get a better view of the goings-on. Then, in the distance, a mighty roar from the crowd followed by cheering and singing, growing louder and nearer by the minute. Slowly the procession of tramcars wound its way up from the Docks to Below Bar, with men smiling and waving and looking just a little dazed at the warmth of their reception. In the crowd there were already some eyes a trifle too bright from goodwill bought in a bottle, but everyone's gaze was upon the open trams as they crept slowly under the mediaeval

Below: Knifeboard open-top Southampton tramcar No 45 (built in 1903 for use through the Bargate) was sold for preservation in 1948. It is now restored to active use at Crich Tramway Museum, Derbyshire./*Author*

Bargate amid the tumultuous din. Five long, costly years of conflict in Flanders and the Low Countries had bought peace once more for Europe – the war to end all wars was over and this was 1919!

How exciting it must have seemed all those years ago; I can remember dimly the celebrations that followed the conclusion of World War II in 1945, when effigies were burned atop bonfires in the streets and I was allowed to stay up very, very late for once in my life. An air of jubilation was mingled with one of expectancy for the morrow, birth of a new 'Golden Age'? We know, you know, that the peace has been almost harder than the war. They didn't call it inflation then, but increases in the price of basic commodities were as difficult to sustain in the 1920s as they are in the computer age. With all the men coming home to be demobbed there were problems of employment, of adjustment to a more peaceful role as a civilian. The women, too, had to adjust to the return of their menfolk. Many of them had taken over their jobs during the war, driving trams or taking fares, a far cry from playing with the children in the nursery or staying at home with the cooking and the sewing. Not yet accustomed to the vote, women were to begin their long march to emancipation through the 'Roaring Twenties'.

There was no golden age of plenty, no crock of gold at the end of the rainbow. For Britain, newly released from the burden of a war in Europe, there was the unique problem of peace at home. Jobs, better living conditions, better pay, the Jarrow march, the General Strike; all these were to come between the triumphant Tommy and the peace he had fought for, a turbulent backcloth before which our transport began to throb with a restless urgency and speed never achieved before nor since. The 1920s were a cauldron, smoking and hot, yet somehow gentlemanly and restrained to allow the white-heat of new ideas to cool into practical commonsense and achievement. Before the war the motor bus had been a novelty, almost a joke beside the solid reliability of the trams – which seemed to have been around for ever. But London's buses had been to war: they had learned a lot from the need to transport men and equipment surely to the battle-front. Other countries, too, had learned new tricks and soon vehicles manufactured in Scandinavia, Europe and America were finding their way into Britain's daily life as competition for the new highways of peace grew ever more intense. In Hampshire the local firm of Thornycroft began to supply municipal fleets in both Portsmouth and Southampton with 'J' type chassis, to provide feeder services as a cheaper extension of route than laying expensive tram tracks. But, for a time, the buses remained just a poor relation to the trams, for the rough state of many roads together with the basic springing and solid tyres of those early vehicles made them unsuited to lengthy journeys. But it was to be a different tale once they changed to pneumatics. . . .

Left: Portsmouth in the 1920s. The organ grinder, or hurdy-gurdy man was a familiar sight in any large town./*The News, Portsmouth*

Right: The garage and coach-building firm of Wadham Bros had its premises in London Road, Waterlooville.
/*C. H. T. Marshall*

Below: Covered-top through Southampton's Bargate. Percy Baker's domed-roof car No 12 successfully negotiated the mediaeval arch in 1923.
/*Southern Newspapers Ltd*

In Southampton a service of horse-trams had begun in 1879. After 19 years of private enterprise the system was purchased by the Corporation, subject to the inevitable lawsuit over the price! In 1900 the first section of electrified tramway opened to Shirley and was progressively extended over the years. Apart from a very brief flirtation with motor buses in 1901, the Corporation stuck assiduously to trams until 1919, when some Thornycroft double-deckers were taken into service. Tramcar design in Southampton was dominated by the spectre of the Bargate, with knifeboard cars being the order of the day for many years. Not all cars were intended to use the route to the Docks, however, so that covered-top double-deck trams made their appearance in Southampton nine years before the first examples were seen in neighbouring Portsmouth – excluding the unique steam tram 'Lifu', which belonged to Provincial. But it was not until 1923 that covered cars began to be used through the Bargate, following a most ingenious design by the Acting Manager and Engineer, Percy Baker. These domed-roof trams were most distinctive and his final examples – known as 'Pullmans' – were built at Portswood in 1930 for the last extension to the tramway along Burgess Road to Swaythling. In fact, Portswood Depot built many bus and tram bodies for their own system, but the Corporation was not beyond purchasing secondhand vehicles in time of need – such as covered-top ex-London County Council trams in 1918.

Our first visit to Southampton closes as we follow the fortunes of its only 'Toast-rack' car No. 2. Rebuilt from a war-weary open-top tram, it re-entered service in 1916 only to be sold to Portsmouth Corporation Tramways three years later, where it was often used for illuminated displays.

12

2
First Chink in the Armour

It has been said, with some truth, that there is nothing so permanent as something which is 'temporary'. When the trams in Portsmouth became overcrowded following the cessation of hostilities, it may well be that aldermen and councillors agreed to the purchase of ten motor buses as a prompt means of overcoming the problem until further tram lines might be laid and tramcars acquired. The municipal system had not then 'come of age', being established in 1901 after the right had been exercised to take over private tramway undertakings within the town boundaries. The ten buses were open-top double-deckers: a local garage and coachbuilding firm, Wadhams at Waterlooville, built their 34-seat bodies on Thornycroft 'J' chassis, these being delivered to the Corporation Tramways in 1919. Their duties were to inaugurate a route from Devonshire Avenue to St Mary's Road via the Dockyard and Arundel Street, laying the foundations of what was to become Service C and D during the trolley bus period followed by extension to Havant as the 143 route in more recent times.

Though the reign of those Thornycroft 'J's was to last only ten years, their mark has

Below: Bodywork for Portsmouth's first Thornycroft double-deck buses was supplied by Wadham Bros. Some of the new vehicles are posed outside 'The Heroes' at Waterlooville prior to delivery in 1919. */C. H. T. Marshall*

been indelibly fixed in Portsmouth's history. After some years of heavy usage, the opportunity arose to obtain some second-hand bodies of basically similar pattern from London General Omnibus Company, which was replacing its famous AEC 'B'-series design of 1910 by more modern designs during the mid-1920s. Thus Dodson in turn displaced Wadham in the last two or three years that the 'J' type saw service: the former body was more angular in its appearance but, despite a decade and a half of use in peace and war, it was more robust as befitted a solid-tyred vehicle. From my grandfather's copy of Thornycroft's illustrated Instruction Book it appears that the 'J' chassis was equipped with a 30hp 4-cylinder petrol engine with worm-driven back axle, capable of a gross load of 3¾ tons.

Right: A less-familiar aspect of Thornycroft 'J' BK 2986 at North End depot in 1928. Shortly after, No 10 was laid aside for preservation by Portsmouth Corporation Tramways – it was later renumbered 1. */Portsmouth City Archivist*

Below: One of the English Electric covered-top tramcars on the traverser at North End depot in the early 1920s./*Portsmouth City Archivist*

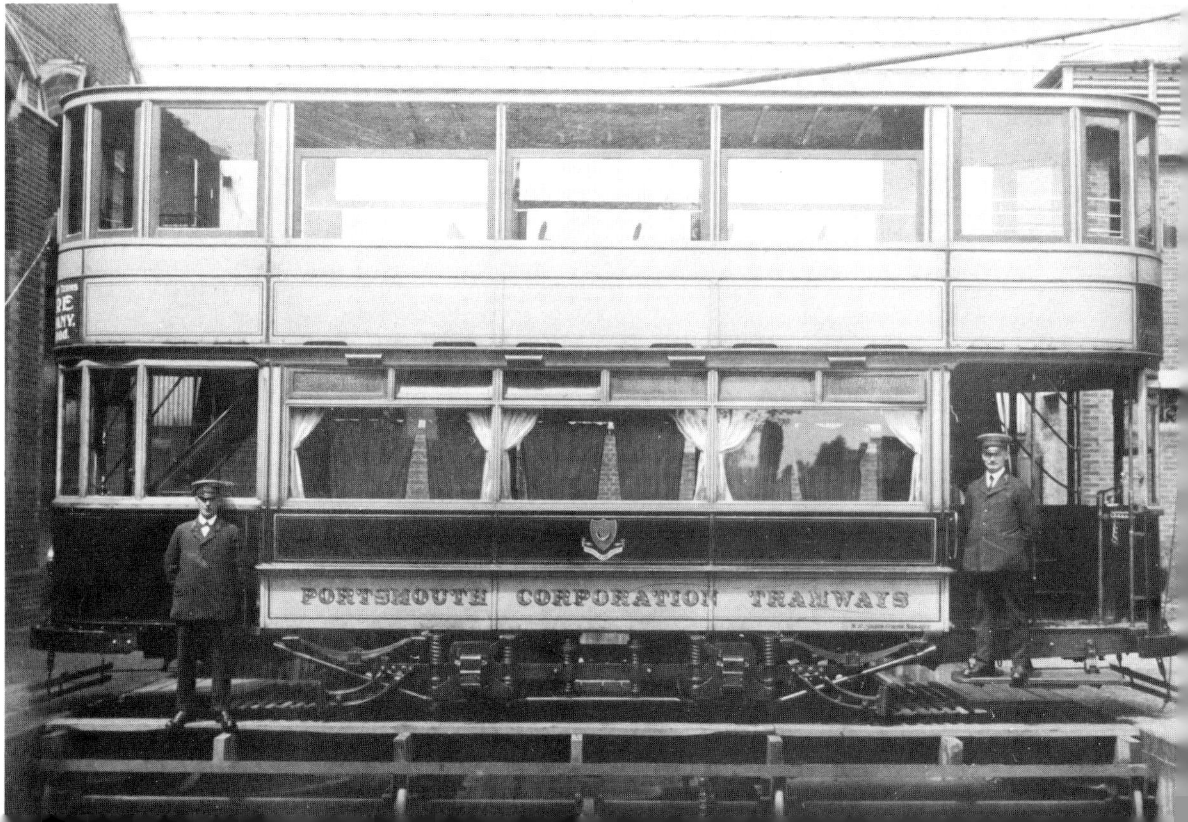

Today, thanks to the great foresight exercised by the Passenger Transport Department of the new City of Portsmouth (on being raised to that status in 1927), succeeding generations of Portsmuthians can enjoy the sight of one of those earliest motor buses, for No. 10 was taken out of service when ten years old and salted away until suitably venerable. (I shall return to it again in the conclusion). Yet, although the first buses did not outlive the trams in ordinary service, for a dozen covered-top cars were delivered in 1921, their decade in use caused much heart-searching as to the future of tracked urban transport. The flexibility of buses sounded the death-knell of Portsmouth's tramways, even if it was not quite time to nail down the coffin lid. With much new building of residential properties in areas like Copnor and North End, to lay new tram tracks to serve these districts at a time of national stringency was rather like asking for a hundred miles of new motorway in the 1970s; failure to do so was both short-sighted yet understandable.

Another five years were to elapse before any further motor buses were purchased. In 1924 five little Guy 'Toastracks' were taken into stock and used on seafront services, while the same year saw the arrival of a first consignment of Dennis single-deckers originally intended for one-man operation! More Dennis buses of various models and bodybuilders were obtained until 1929 and to them fell the doubtful distinction of first tramway replacement vehicles, when one service in each direction was withdrawn over the section between Fratton Bridge and The Strand (having become routes 19 and 20) in 1928. But perhaps more indicative of the shape of things to come was the arrival of a striking octet of covered-top double-deck motor buses in 1927. These were the vast three-axle Karrier WL6 models with 60-seat bodies by Brush; not only did they sport pneumatic tyres, and roofs, but they positively dwarfed everything else in the fleet. However, whereas the tiny Toastracks and several Dennis buses remained in harness until the outbreak of war in 1939, a respectable

Below: Built entirely at Guildford, Dennis 2½ ton 26 seater No 23(TP 751) is inspected by members of the Tramways Committee before entering service in April 1925./*Portsmouth City Archivist*

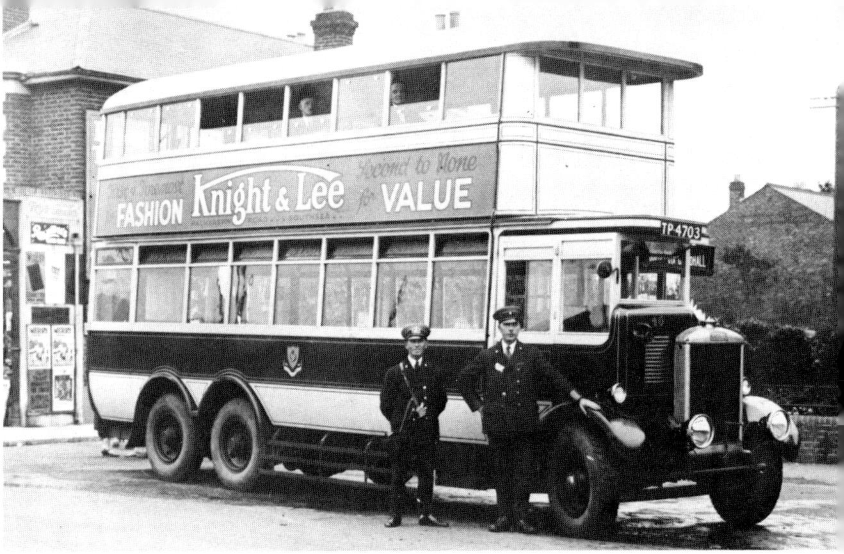

Top right: There was a sudden craze for high-capacity three-axle covered-top double-deckers in both Portsmouth and Southampton during the late 1920s. The latter purchased Thornycrofts while the former chose the Karrier WL6 model. No 40, with Brush body, lays over at Cosham railway station before its next journey to South Parade Pier via Guildhall.
/Portsmouth City Archivist

Centre right: Brush-bodied Karrier WL6 No 42 (TP 4705) follows the tramlines from Portsbridge towards Cosham on service B in 1930. Behind the bus can be seen the contours of Hilsea Lines.
/The News, Portsmouth

Below: Bodywork contrasts on the Thornycroft BC chassis are illustrated by 71 (TP 8094) with Hall Lewis design (right) while 72 (TP 8096) features Wadhams' style. The buses are picking up dockyard workers outside Unicorn Gate, both dating from 1929. The wall behind the buses conceals a single-line railway from Portsmouth & Southsea station.
/Portsmouth City Archivist

Above: 'The Coach and Horses' at Hilsea in earlier guise, about 1929. / *The News, Portsmouth*

lifespan in any period but worthy of Methuselah in those days, the lumbering Karriers did not make double figures in service despite the injection of a further half dozen with English Electric bodywork in 1928. To be charitable they were rather ahead of their time so far as size was concerned, since many city roads were narrow with tortuous bends, to say nothing of the hazards of interlaced tram tracks and cobbled setts. . . . It remains a fact that no more double-deck motor buses joined the fleet until the 1930s, by which time the Karriers were outclassed in terms of everything except sheer volume. Few pictures of them seem to exist but then, 50 years ago, both cameras and bus enthusiasts were less plentiful than they are today. Two single-deck Karriers had also seen service during this period.

Right at the end of the decade, Portsmouth turned back to Thornycrofts for some 32-seat single-deckers with bodies by Hall Lewis and Wadham. So the 1920s were not noted for any real attempt at standardisation, although a steady trickle of Dennis buses had been coming down from Guildford. No doubt the rumblings that had been going on about the future of the trams must have made longterm planning difficult, particularly in the context of the nation's economic problems. There had been talk of rail-less electric vehicles, but we shall hear more of those in a later chapter. The tramcar in Portsmouth had just one ace left in the pack.

3
Over the Hill and Far Away

When Portsmouth Town Council decided to exercise its option (available under the Tramways Act 1870) to acquire those parts of the Portsmouth Street Tramways Company that lay within the town boundaries and, by agreement, beyond them to Cosham, it was clear to the Board of the parent concern (Provincial Tramways Co Ltd) that its future in the Portsmouth area lay in developing routes beyond the island of Portsea. 'Municipalisation' took place on 1 January 1901, but Provincial's plans for a route from Cosham to Horndean were already well advanced.

Two years later the Portsdown and Horndean Light Railway commenced operation of a single route northwards from Cosham (where there was an interchange platform with the Corporation trams), crossing the LSWR Fareham-Portcreek Junction line just west of Cosham station on a girder bridge, to ascend Portsdown Hill past Queen Alexandra Hospital and Widley

Below: Before urbanisation — Portsdown Hill and Fort Widley, with Light Railway cars on double-track section north of Cosham./*C. H. T. Marshall*

Lane to 'The George' at the summit. The track (to the 'standard' gauge of 4ft 7¾in) followed London Road – now the A3 – through the villages of Purbrook and Waterlooville, after which it became a roadside reservation on the eastern verge through Cowplain to a terminus at the top of a short hill down into Horndean – opposite the 'Good Intent', now a Schooner Inn. A three-road depot was constructed at Hart Plain, Cowplain, which survived until the 1950s as a depot for Foden lorries. Today the site is occupied by a supermarket. Electrified from the very beginning, the Light Railway service was maintained by a modest fleet of double-deck open-top cars, numbered 1 to 16, painted in the traditional emerald green and cream livery of Provincial. After a number of early disputes with the Corporation over the cost of electricity from the Portsmouth power station in Vivash Road and over running-rights between Cosham and Portsdown, the Light Railway settled down to a relatively prosperous and peaceful existence for a period of 32 years.

With the war ended in 1919, we have already seen that the demand for transport in the Portsmouth area was becoming intense. A service of buses over Portsdown Hill was being run by the Southsea Tourist Company, avoiding the need to change trams at Cosham, so proposals were put forward to permit through-running by

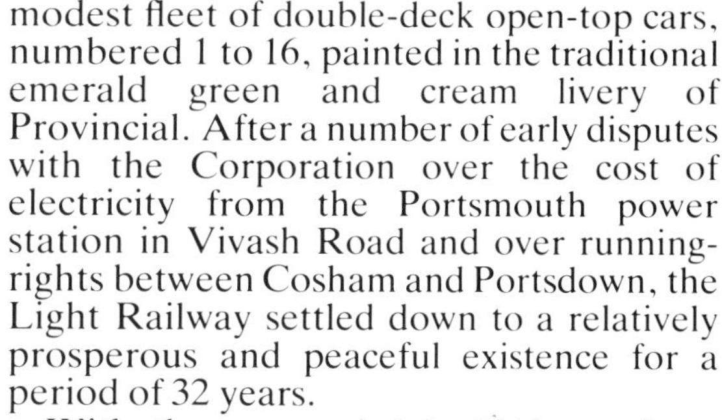

Left: Before the Light Railway was completed, single-deck cars were towed to the depot at Cowplain by steam traction-engine for their upper-decks to be added prior to electrification. The strange entourage passes Waterlooville about 1902./*C. H. T. Marshall*

Below: As Light Railway cars did not commence operations till after lunch on Sundays, Hambledon huntsmen and their hounds were able to use the entire road through the centre of Waterlooville during the earlier part of the day./*C. H. T. Marshall*

'green cars' between Horndean and the Guildhall. Approval was given and the through service began in August 1924, at a cost of 9d. In ensuing years the service was progressively extended to Palmerston Road and South Parade Pier, with Light Railway cars travelling initially by way of North End, Kingston Crescent and Commercial Road. Later their route was altered to travel via Kingston Road and Lake Road but, as the Corporation progressively abandoned its own tramway system, in the final year of the Light Railway's existence through trams reverted to their original route past the Town Hall (now the Guildhall) to South Parade Pier.

For one season only, in 1925, it appears that the green trams ran to Clarence Pier on Sundays and Bank Holidays since, at that stage, through-running had not been authorised beyond Palmerston Road to South Parade. Also in that year, possibly in imitation of the Corporation's purchase of a secondhand open single-deck car from Southampton, the Light Railway acquired a similar tram from Provincial's subsidiary at Grimsby for use on occasional services to Clarence Pier. This became No 17 on the Light Railway, but its use was limited because it proved to be too long for certain curves on the section to Palmerston Road and it ceased to appear in subsequent years. According to the late S. E. Harrison in his book *The Tramways of Portsmouth*, this car had been designed by H. Orme White – of whom more anon in connection with the other Provincial subsidiary in the Solent area, which became the Gosport and Fareham Omnibus Company after abandonment of its tramways system in 1929. Several of the Gosport cars were transferred to the Light Railway both to replace and augment some of the original fleet. Former Gosport cars which replaced Light Railway trams could be recognised by their lack of reversed staircases.

After full through-running was permitted to South Parade Pier from 19 April 1927, the original route mileage of 5¾ was extended to become just over 10½ miles from Horndean.

Below: Leaving the siding (loop) at Waterlooville, Light Railway car No 13 heads south for the interchange platform at Cosham on single-track street tramway. */C. H. T. Marshall*

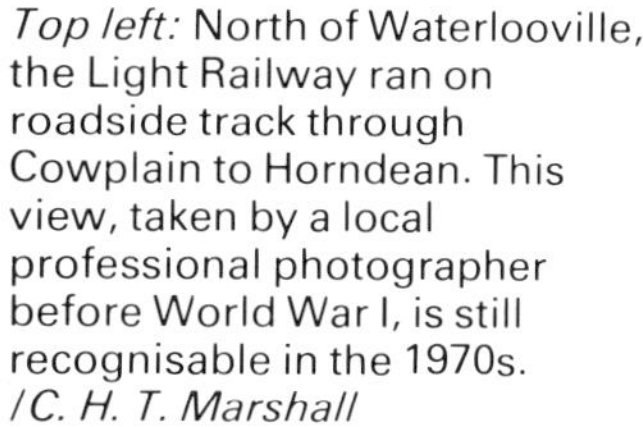

Top left: North of Waterlooville, the Light Railway ran on roadside track through Cowplain to Horndean. This view, taken by a local professional photographer before World War I, is still recognisable in the 1970s.
/*C. H. T. Marshall*

Centre left: The Southsea Tourist Company was a force to be reckoned with in the scramble for business after World War I. At first Dennis charabancs were operated like BK 2130.
/*D. Fereday Glenn collection*

Below: The famous 'Tramway Arms' at the junction of Lake Road and Kingston Road, Portsmouth. For a few years from 1927 the 'green trams' were allowed to travel through to South Parade Pier via Lake Road but in this view Corporation car No 74 shows Strand on its blinds.
/*The News, Portsmouth*

4
Birth of the 'Southern'

After the demands of war, railway companies throughout Britain were in need of fresh rolling-stock and renewed capital investment. Many were too small to raise this from their own resources but, following some inter-company cooperation during the period of hostilities, it was inevitable that mergers of the more modest concerns should take place fairly soon. That the extent of the Grouping was so great (when it came) only serves to illustrate for us, 60 years on, how dire was their situation after the Armistice.

The London & South Western Railway was the first to bring the new iron road to the Portsmouth area, though this was not a direct line but a branch to Gosport owing to the nature of the fortifications on the island of Portsea. In fact it was the London, Brighton & South Coast Company that first succeeded in breeching those defences, to extend their line from Havant into Portsmouth in 1847, closely followed by the South Western with another branch (off the Gosport line) at Fareham running eastward through Cosham to join the Brighton line at Portcreek Junction in 1848. The two companies managed to agree on joint operation, though this happy accord was rudely shaken by the South Western's Direct line from

London when this pierced the South Downs and linked up Godalming with Havant in 1859. But whereas Gosport's railway remained forever a branch, with various sub-branches to the Victualling Yard, Stokes Bay and (from Fort Brockhurst) to Lee-on-the-Solent, the Portsmouth line was extended and expanded to terminate ultimately at the Harbour station. This adjoined the pontoon for both Gosport launches and the rail-owned ferries to the Isle of Wight, which made for an easier crossing to Ryde than from either South Parade or Clarence Piers, for neither the Southsea rail branch (from Fratton) nor the tramway from Portsmouth Town station were best suited to interchange traffic for a variety of reasons. The latter became part of Portsmouth Corporation Tramways, while the former branch survived in a moribund state following the outbreak of war in 1914 until the 'marriage' creating the Southern Railway in 1923.

The Naval Dockyard had its own internal railway tracks from an early date, with a short branch crossing Edinburgh Road to link it with the main line at Portsmouth Town for interchange traffic. On completion of the Harbour Extension in 1876 a second link with the Dockyard was established, with the primary object of serving what became South Railway Jetty – this was noted mostly for VIP traffic or to connect with troopships berthed there, whereas the earlier line's purpose was predominantly for freight and naval supplies.

The Southsea (later East Southsea) branch had opened in 1885 as a local venture to serve the needs of that essentially residential district. Connection with the main line was by way of a reverse junction at Fratton, but it never achieved great success with through traffic despite carriages being attached or detached at the junction. It was another example of cooperation between the South Western and Brighton companies, who agreed to operate it on alternate years. When electrification of the town's tramways occurred, the true status of the branch was recognised by the opening of two wooden halts at Jessie Road and Albert Road, coinciding with the employment of a novel steam Railmotor on purely local traffic in 1903. Though built of double track, one line had, by this time, become merely a siding. Even the elaborate terminal station at Granada Road became obsolete, for a simple halt platform similar to those in use at intermediate places was built out in the yard and sufficed for the domestic needs of the Railmotors. All traffic effectively ceased in 1914, though my father recalls its existence during his boyhood at Whitwell Road in Southsea.

Within the Solent area before 1923, railways included the following 'main' lines:

London (Victoria) to Portsmouth via Arundel, Chichester and Havant.
Brighton to Portsmouth via Chichester and

Below left: Now preserved in York Museum, Adams 4–4–0 No 563 is representative of the London & South Western Railway express passenger locomotives designed in the late-19th century. It was displayed at Eastleigh Works Open Day in 1957, together with a Marsh Atlantic 4–4–2./*Author*

Below: Representative of pre-Grouping LBSCR motive-power, Stroudley 'Terrier' 0–6–0T No 663 restarts a Hayling branch train from Langston./*Lens of Sutton*

Havant (the first into Portsmouth, as related above).

London (Waterloo) to Portsmouth via Guildford and Havant (the 1859 'Direct' line referred to above).

London (Waterloo) to Portsmouth via Eastleigh and Fareham (the first LSWR route into Portsmouth).

London (Waterloo) to Gosport via Eastleigh (or, after 1903, alternatively via Alton and the Meon Valley line to Fareham).

London (Waterloo) to Southampton via Eastleigh, continuing to Bournemouth etc.

There were also a number of branch or secondary lines:

(Portsmouth –) Fareham – Netley – St Denys (– Southampton – Salisbury).

Havant – Langston – Hayling Island.

Botley – Bishop's Waltham.

Brockenhurst – Lymington Town – Lymington Pier (for Yarmouth).

Fort Brockhurst – Lee-on-the-Solent.

Petersfield – Midhurst.

Chichester – Midhurst (– Petworth– Pulborough).

Romsey – Fullerton Jct – Andover Town – Andover Jct.

Fullerton Jct – Hurstbourne.

Shawford Jct – Winchester Chesil (– Newbury etc). This was the Didcot, Newbury and Southampton line that was absorbed by the Great Western Railway.

24

Finally, there were private railway lines in Portsmouth Dockyard, at Portsmouth Gasworks, Royal Naval Victualling Yard (Gosport), Bedenham, Netley Hospital, Hilsea Ordnance Depot and at Hamble. Most of these were connected with defence, the remainder with industry. In addition, a number of through-running agreements existed which brought through coaches or strange engines to Solent coast resorts from time to time.

From 1 January 1923 virtually every line mentioned above became part of the Southern Railway which owned, despite its being the smallest of the 'Big Four', an empire that stretched from Kent to Cornwall. The other railway was the Great Western; this was the only system to retain its title under the Grouping arrangements, apart from certain minor systems not then absorbed and beyond the scope of this volume. GWR trains ran to Portsmouth from Reading and to Southampton Terminus (formerly Southampton Docks station) from the Newbury line via Winchester Chesil or from Cheltenham via Swindon and Andover over the former Midland & South Western Junction route. No changes of note affected the position throughout the 1920s.

Nominally independent railways in the Isle of Wight were all absorbed into the Southern Railway in 1923, which then began to standardise operations using suitable surplus suburban tank engines and rolling-stock from the mainland. In view of the excellent coverage of the whole subject of the Isle of Wight railways in other works, I shall confine myself to a brief look at them later, in so far as they were the logical final destination of railway-owned steamers across the Solent from Portsmouth and Lymington, together with Red Funnel services from Southampton.

Above left: Joint Railcar No 1 for the Southsea branch from Fratton, after rebuilding in 1903 with improved boiler. The locomotive portion was painted LSWR green and the carriage in Brighton chocolate and cream. It was broken up at Eastleigh in 1919. */National Railway Museum, Crown Copyright*

Left: Southsea Steam Railmotor No 2 in original condition at Fratton station soon after its introduction – an attempt to compete with the newly-electrified street tramways of Portsmouth./*Councillor F.A.J.Emery-Wallis*

Below left: The unique double-arm signal at Edinburgh Road Crossing on the Portsmouth Dockyard goods branch, showing original timber slotted-post, looking towards Unicorn Gate./*Author*

Below: South Western H12 class steam Railmotor No 1 spent most of its short life working the Bishops Waltham branch from Botley, between 1904 and 1916. This early picture shows the substantial terminus with a wonderful assortment of station bric a brac and full signalling./*National Railway Museum, Crown Copyright*

5
How Gosport's Trams Became Gosport's Buses

On the basis of 'last in, first out', the most recently electrified subsidiary of the Provincial Tramways 'empire' – the Gosport and Fareham Tramways, as they were known locally – had the shortest lifespan of all electric tramways in the Solent area. Its narrow-gauge horse-trams of 1882 graduated to a fullblown electrified system on the 'standard' gauge of 4ft 7¾in in 1905, yet still officially called the Portsmouth Street Tramways Company, despite being on the opposite side of the Harbour and physically unconnected either with the municipalised Portsmouth lines or the newly built Portsdown and Horndean Light Railway. Sensibly, electrification provided the opportunity to widen the track gauge from the three foot of horse-tram days to Provincial's 'standard' width, which had the added virtue of being able to accommodate railway wagons built to the traditional 4ft 8½in gauge, since their flanges could run on the bottom of the groove in the track with tyres clear of the rail surface. This facility became reality during World War I, when a short goods line connected the LSWR Gosport branch with a Naval Yard at Bedenham using the tram tracks for a brief distance in the process, though this practice ceased

Right: Grandfather's office at 88 High Street, Gosport – above the Gosport & Alverstoke Electric Lighting Company Ltd, another Provincial subsidiary.
/R. Brown collection

Left: One of the earliest motor buses in Gosport, this Darracq (BO 461) is believed to have originated in Cardiff with another Provincial subsidiary in 1909, before working the Lee-on-the-Solent service./*Gosport Museum*

Below: An early picture of the Gosport & Fareham Tramways. Car No 8 pauses at the railway viaduct in Fareham, before proceeding up Portland Street. Graffiti was not unknown before World War I! /*D. Fereday Glenn collection*

Bottom: Car No 11 bound for Fareham at Walpole Road junction. Trams for Bury Cross continued past the building on the left towards Stoke Road. /*D. Fereday Glenn collection*

soon after the war ended. However, it is interesting to note that survival of a truncated part of the old Gosport railway as far as Bedenham, at the time of writing, is entirely due to Ministry of Defence needs in this day and age.

S. E. Harrison, writing of the Gosport system in his book *The Tramways of Portsmouth*, states that my grandfather (J. Fereday Glenn) drove the very first electric tram into Gosport from Fareham station on 20 December 1905, running via Brockhurst and Forton Road. Nearly a year was to pass before the second route from Bury Cross to the Ferry via Stoke Road was opened. Thereafter, despite attempts to extend the Fareham line through Portchester to Cosham (to form a physical link with the Portsdown and Horndean Light Railway) in pursuit of powers obtained under an Act of Parliament in 1903, the system remained limited to just two routes. One is tempted to conclude that this may well have influenced its decision to abandon trams in favour of buses at an earlier date than other local tramway undertakings, for the Provincial Company had a long history of ancillary operations such as hire cars, charabancs, hearses, wedding carriages and omnibuses! A motor bus had been used on an experimental service from Bury Cross to Lee-on-the-Solent in about 1905, being replaced later by a more regular operation from Brockhurst to Lee-on-the-Solent, which

Above: In case it should rain . . . Thornycroft 'J' charabanc No 1 (AA 5301) poses with its hood up, flanked by Driver Cutland and his mate.
/*D. Fereday Glenn collection*

must have brought little comfort to the railway running between those same two points. Could it possibly have been prompted by the South Western's intransigence over the proposed extension to Portchester and Cosham?

Apart from employing women as both drivers and conductors on the trams during the war, my grandfather's term of office as Engineer and Manager of the Gosport and Fareham Tramways appears in retrospect to have been remarkably tranquil – he had been appointed to the Light Railway in 1903 and held the same posts in both companies concurrently from 1905 until 1924. Electricity for the Gosport trams was obtained from the Gosport and Alverstoke Electric Lighting Co Ltd – another Provincial subsidiary – which also supplied domestic current to the two local authorities, so no problems like those of early days on the Light Railway were experienced here. A total of 22 open-top double-deck cars in the usual Provincial livery provided the service, additional short workings on the Fareham route as far as Brockhurst supplementing

the normal 15 minute headway from the ferry to Fareham station. A 10 minute service operated on the Stoke Road route, cars showing 'The Avenue' when working to Bury Cross. The depot and power station were at Hoeford, one mile south of Fareham, where all repairs, repainting and reconstruction were carried out. A small fleet of Thornycroft 'J' charabanc single-deck motor buses was built up, which were popular for private hire outings once peace was declared. Parties from the 'Royal Arms' and Camper & Nicholson Limited are known to have chartered these vehicles, a group of football supporters venturing as far as Weymouth on one occasion! With their solid tyres and rudimentary canvas hoods, passengers on those 'charas' must have been hardy folk.

Grandfather retired on 31 March 1924, being presented with a handsome clock as a token of the regard in which he was held by his employees. It was said that his decision to retire early was prompted by a disagreement over policy to abandon the trams; if this was the case, his foresight was commendable in view of the energy crisis over oil that rocked Britain 50 years later. At all events, in 1929 a further Act of Parliament allowed the Portsmouth Street Tramways Company to change its name to the Gosport & Fareham Omnibus Company, abandon

28

trams and substitute motor buses, all of which objectives were achieved by the end of the year. The Fareham route was cut back to Ann's Hill prior to final closure, so that only empty cars ran to and from Hoeford Depot in the last weeks. Car No 8 is reputed to have made the ultimate journey to Ann's Hill before being transferred, along with six of its fellows, to Cowplain on the Light Railway for further service or as spares. Six more went to Provincial's Grimsby subsidiary, the rest being scrapped. The traditional Provincial 'belt' (or garter) continued to appear on replacement buses for another 40 years !

One can only conjecture whether success in achieving the proposed link between Fareham and Cosham could have saved the trams. The indecent haste with which they were abandoned all over Britain (as compared with Europe and elsewhere) would probably have caused their demise sooner or later, but many occupants of cars crawling nose-to-tail in traffic jams each weekday from Gosport to Fareham or in and out of Portsmouth today, regardless of motorways, might have other views! One irony is that Gosport & Fareham Omnibus Company now operates a bus beyond Fareham to new housing estates at Portchester – the 'South Western' must be turning in its grave. . . .

Above: An interesting assortment of single- and double-deck buses in Gosport about 1918. The 'J' type Thornycroft on the far right shows destinations to Fareham, Titchfield, Locks Heath and Warsash. /*R. Brown collection*

Below: An early pair of Dennis appliances formed the Gosport Fire Brigade in 1929./*The News, Portsmouth*

Bottom: Gosport's proximity to the sea cannot be doubted!/*Gosport Museum*

6
The Founding of the 'Bus Barons'

Whilst tentative measures were being tried in Portsmouth by the Corporation with its first ten motor buses and, across the harbour in 'Turk Town', Provincial had a small fleet of Thornycrofts as ancillaries to their trams, a substantial number of small operators of motor vehicles had come and gone since the turn of the century all along the southern coast. These were mostly family concerns of horse-bus or cab operators, or who used their vehicles as lorries at night and for passengers by day. But, during and after World War I, amalgamations and takeovers were beginning to establish the first major omnibus operators as we know them today. Very often these 'mergers' involved the transfer of a handful of vehicles, all the staff and a small office or parking

space – plus the all important licences! Rivalry was of the essence and contemporary accounts have a swashbuckling flavour almost akin to the adventures of Robin Hood. Although early attempts to establish services in 1907 between Bognor and Southsea and also between Portsmouth and Hambledon by the Sussex Motor Road Car Company failed due to the company's insolvency, after the formation of Southdown Motor Services Ltd at Brighton in 1915 it was not long before fresh efforts were being made in this direction. By 1920 Southdown had established what was to become the famous service 31 between Brighton and Southsea – with the trend in takeovers only just beginning!

Just as one of the major Solent bus companies was based at Brighton, some 50 miles from Portsmouth along the Sussex shore, so another omnibus giant had its roots in Bournemouth at about the same period. In 1916 Bournemouth & District Motor Services Ltd was created, extending its influence to Southampton in 1920 after having gained physical access into Bournemouth, thanks to the support of the Borough of Lymington the previous year. Very soon its name was changed to the one we are all familiar with today – Hants & Dorset Motor Services Ltd – and progress throughout the decade was marked by many small concerns being absorbed in much the same way as with Southdown. The two major Hampshire constituents of today's National Bus Company had been formed and firmly established in their respective areas by 1920. It is also interesting to note that they were linked in those early days, too, since both Mr W. F. French and Mr Sidney Garcke were involved on the Boards of both companies. The former even became Chairman of each!

In view of the foregoing, it is not perhaps entirely surprising that some joint services came into being between Southdown and Hants & Dorset during the 1920s to the north and west of Fareham. But, after several years frenetic activity, each settled down to consolidate its own particular area: Southdown withdrew to a western boundary at Fareham (with an hourly exception extended to Titchfield and Warsash after absorbing Fuger's service in later years) while Hants & Dorset no longer ventured eastward into Portsmouth on normal stage services. Special through-fares facilities were maintained, however, not only between these two operators but also with their northern neighbour, Aldershot and District. After acquiring some land in Portsmouth, Southdown was able to build a depot and offices at Hyde Park Road in 1923 – these premises are still owned and used by the Company (now mostly for coaches) although the road has been renamed Winston Churchill Avenue within the last decade. An acquisition of major importance to Southdown was their purchase of the Southsea Tourist Company in 1925, which had become a thorn in the flesh of the tramway operators with its services beyond Portsdown Hill. A large fleet of Dennis vehicles was involved but, in addition to their bus services, Southsea Tourist brought with them a thriving coaching business that was particularly attractive to Southdown. In a later chapter we shall see how Hants & Dorset adopted a similar policy towards coaches and excursion licenses in the 1930s. The development of pneumatic tyres, improved suspension and more standardised chassis helped to encourage the coaching side to become something of a 'growth industry'. Some of the Leyland N and G7 charabanc vehicles built with solid tyres were converted to pneumatics and rebodied as open-top double-deck buses in the late 1920s, to prolong their useful lives in an era of rapid technical improvement. Gradually, too, the plethora of vehicle variety began to abate in favour of greater standardisation. Both speed and

Left: After six years as a solid-tyred charabanc, Leyland G7 CD 7045 was rebodied as an open-top double-decker by Short Bros in 1928. After spending 35 years with Gosport & Fareham Omnibus Company, it was re-acquired by Southdown in 1970 for restoration to its late-1920s condition, as No 135./*Author*

safety increased with the provision of four-wheel brakes in the latter part of the decade, but many of the older chassis survived into the next either on lesser duties with their original purchaser or, after resale, to any one of the myriads of small operators who continued to appear until the introduction of the Road Traffic Act 1930, which vested powers of licensing in the hands of regional Traffic Commissioners, whose ruling was final. But in order to make their judgment, it was sometimes necessary to consult with the regular crews to establish exactly precise routes and terminal points of some of the services.

Before leaving the 'Roaring Twenties', it might be pertinent to mention just a tiny selection of the chassis makes and models that contributed to the great leap forward in public road transport during the decade. Many had but a few years of glory before being swallowed up and lost in the fierce competition for new and improved designs. In the little pocket *ABC Guide to Southdown*, produced in 1951 by Ian Allan Ltd as one of their first publications on buses, one reads of Scout, Caledon, 'CB', McCurd and Ensign; more famous makes that have since vanished included Unic, Vulcan, Maudslay and Tilling-Stevens – the last named being particularly noted for its petrol-electrics. There is mention of Commer and Daimler, Berliet, Chevrolet and Fiat but – steadily and increasingly – the variety of Leyland models began to influence the trend towards greater uniformity and longer life. For while the PLSC1 and PLSC3 Lion four-cylinder single-deck models did not find favour with Southdown – they were popular when new with Hants & Dorset and found a ready purchaser in later years at Provincial – yet the influence of the new double-deck Titan model with its lower chassis level, four-wheel brakes and semi-floating axle cannot be over-emphasised. With servo-assisted braking and a powerful 6.8 litre six-cylinder petrol engine, Leyland had a winner on its hands that was to become the standard by which other designs were judged for the next quarter of a century. Nor was it slow to utilise the new diesel engine being evolved at this time – steadily it was to gain in popularity throughout the 1930s before becoming the norm thereafter. It is the more creditable that Leyland's existing models at the 'heavy' end of its range should have been capable of adaptation to the new technology with almost no obvious sign, for we shall see that its diesel engines were to be offered as an alternative to petrol units on the same chassis! But the battle for supremacy all those years ago was not easily won, for the makers of Guy, Dennis, AEC, Daimler and Bristol were busy establishing a firm hold while new competitors would arise during the next few years. I think it is true to say that the 1920s period was the crucible in which much of our subsequent transport history was cast.

Left: A fascinating study of Fareham bus station in 1930. Hants & Dorset Leyland Lion PLSC1 B132 (TR 2655) waits to leave for Bursledon via Titchfield. The gaunt Wesleyan Methodist Church was demolished in the 1950s, to enlarge the bus station. /*The News, Portsmouth*

Epoch II

1929~1939, Sunshine and Shadows

7
Start of the Railway Revolution

When the Southern Railway opened a new branch line to Fawley from Totton in 1925, there was such a deafening silence of publicity that not even the National Railway Museum can find an official photograph of the proceedings. But if the new amalgam was bashful of its early achievements, we shall see that this trait had soon disappeared by the 1930s. Nor was it the only thing to vanish, for the Depression provided an excuse to offload several unprofitable branch lines in the area. Not all disappeared without trace, for in some instances a freight service continued to operate while buses made good the passenger deficiency by expanding under the auspices of the Road Traffic Act 1930. Just as early inner-suburban passenger services had been dealt a mortal blow by electric trams during the Edwardian era, so the first wave of closures was to sweep away such curiosities as the Basingstoke and Alton Light Railway and the Lee-on-the-Solent line. In neither case was the end immediate – the former had been removed and relaid once already and was to be remembered fondly for all time as a result of the making of Will Hay's *Oh, Mr Porter* for the cinema. Passenger traffic over the three-mile Lee branch did not survive beyond the last day of 1930, though occasional goods trains continued to run

Below: The modest terminus at Lee-on-the-Solent in 1928, with ex-LBSCR 'Terrier' 0–6–0T No B661 in charge of a single 'Gate' auto-trailer./*Gosport Museum*

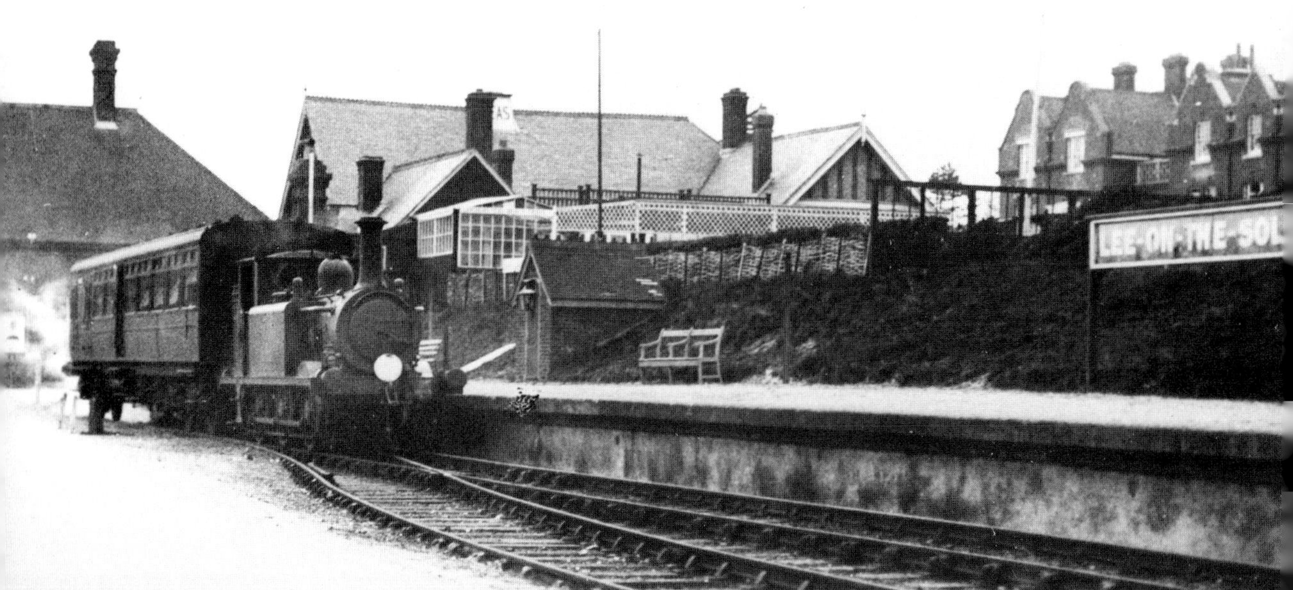

until October 1935. After this, without the magic wit of Will Hay and his friends to immortalise it, the single track from Fort Brockhurst through Gomer Halt, Browndown and Elmore to Lee-on-the-Solent became rusty and forgotten. It was finally ripped up in 1942, when scrap metal was desperately needed for the war effort!

No New Year's resolution saved Bishop's Waltham and its passenger trains ceased from 2 January 1933. However, goods traffic continued to trundle up and down this rural line for almost 30 years – even today a level-crossing gate survives at Waltham and the branch bay and shelter at Botley, but of obscure Durley no trace remains. Both Bishop's Waltham and Lee-on-the-Solent had experienced steam Railmotors in their time, but these scarcely outlived the pair of Joint LSW/LBSC steam Railmotors designed for the Southsea branch, for all were withdrawn by 1920. Yet whereas the Southsea cars soon vanished for ever, the former LSWR Railmotors were returned to service once the rather ineffective power units had been removed and, as push-and-pull trailers, continued to function on branch lines far and wide over the Southern's empire. The last 'gate' set, No 373, was to be found working between Yeovil Town and Yeovil Junction as late as 1958 and rumoured to be intended for preservation, though that worthy aim was frustrated due to a lack of internal communi-

Top: Bishops Waltham in its final days: LMS-designed 2–6–2T No 41214 crosses the A333 with a featherweight goods train on 1 March 1962./*Author*

Above: Bepton road bridge at Midhurst, over which a freight-only connection was maintained between former South Western and Brighton terminals until 1925, whereupon it was strengthened to enable all passenger services to be concentrated at the imposing ex-LBSCR station, beyond the goods yard./*Author*

Left: Pre-1935 view of the junction at Midhurst, showing a Stroudley D1 0–4–2T and auto-train approaching from Chichester, with engine shed and goods yard alongside the Petersfield branch on the right.
/*Lens of Sutton*

cation at the time. Indeed, sadly no example of Southern push-pull stock has survived at all, despite 20 'new' sets being adapted as late as 1960.

Finally, in spite of the 'rationalisation' of stations at Midhurst in 1925 with the closure of the former South Western terminus at Midhurst Common, after which all trains from Petersfield terminated at the handsome LBSCR station almost a mile further east, it was found necessary to cut back on passenger services to Chichester within 10 years. All three intermediate stations between Midhurst and Chichester – Cocking, Singleton and Lavant – remained in business for freight till well after World War II. Like the Lee-on-the-Solent and Gosport branches, those to Midhurst used often to be operated by examples of Stroudley's D1 0-4-2T engines, many of which had been equipped with push-and-pull control gear for motor-train working. In effect, the principles established by the steam Railmotors were perfected by the use of a simple standard tank locomotive of sufficient power – this deficiency being the most common complaint against the integrated Railmotor – coupled to one or two former mainline carriages that were suitably ancient and capable of modification to driving trailers. If locomotive or carriages needed attention, either might be replaced by a similar piece of equipment from the reserve 'pool' so that normal services could be maintained

Top: Classic Brighton architecture at Lavant. Billinton E4 0–6–2T No 32495 prepares to return to Chichester with the goods on 1 July 1959, 24 years after suspension of passenger trains. */Author*

Above: Complete farm removals were possible by train in Southern Railway days. This interesting picture shows cart-horses being led into Horsebox 2502 at a Hampshire station. The clay-ringed chimneys, known as 'Fareham Pots' are noteworthy. */The News, Portsmouth*

Left: Portsmouth & Southsea station before electrification. Super-heated Drummond T9 4–4–0 No 727 backs out of the Low Level while beyond the High Level approach ramp can be seen the former goods yard and dep about 1930. */The News, Portsmouth*

with the minimum of disruption. Likewise, a self-contained locomotive could be used to perform shunting or other tasks in between its normal passenger duties. Perhaps memories of their predecessors' experiences with steam Railmotors caused British Railways to be so chary in experiments with diesel Railbuses – and Southern Region to opt out altogether!

But the biggest change had to wait till 1937. Even before the Grouping there had been experiments with electric traction, both overhead and third-rail. The new Southern Railway decided to standardise on the latter system of current collection at 650V dc, in view of the short-haul nature of the majority of routes likely to be affected. A number of suburban lines were converted to electric traction with new three-car multiple units, together with some rebuilt steam-stock from its South Western and Brighton constituents, but the first main line to be switched to third-rail electrification was from London to Brighton in 1933. This was a major step forward, completely revolutionising the pattern of services, resulting in a continuing increase in patronage, particularly since it became fashionable for business people to live by the South Coast and commute daily to London. In the light of their experiences, Sir Herbert Walker and his team began to look closely at the 'Direct' line to Portsmouth via Guildford and Haslemere.

South of Guildford there were some difficult stretches, including the ascent to Butser Tunnel and ensuing curves thence to Idsworth, making it an arduous route for steam traction with very little opportunity for brisk running. Certain trains were entrusted to the new 'Schools' class three-cylinder 4-4-0 locomotives, which were capable of sustained effort with heavier loads than might be expected to be hauled by the ageing fleet of Drummond 4-4-0s, though these continued to handle slow and semi-fast services thanks to their fuel economy and large-capacity water tenders. By the first months of 1937 preparations were virtually complete and, on 8 March, the first electric train ran from Waterloo to Portsmouth. Unlike the Brighton line, which had favoured six-car corridor sets for its fast trains, the Portsmouth line sets comprised only four coaches but, in addition to providing access between individual coaches within the set, corridor connections were fitted to the outer ends of driving motor-coaches. This enabled staff or passengers to walk throughout an eight- or

Below: A rare view inside the old Portsmouth goods depot adjacent to Portsmouth & Southsea station. This was demolished to make way for empty stock sidings for the new electric trains, being replaced by a modern goods depot at Fratton before World War II. /*The News, Portsmouth*

Above: Commemorating earlier exploits over the Portsmouth Direct before electrification, V class 4–4–0 30929 *Malvern* eases out of the Harbour station past 4-COR 'Nelson' unit No 3131 on 24 February 1957 with a return enthusiasts' special to Waterloo./*Author*

twelve-car formation, a facility that was particularly useful when a buffet or restaurant car was included on the 74½-mile journey. The new stock was code-named 4-COR, 4-BUF or 4-RES according to the facility offered but in later days they became affectionately known, collectively, as 'Nelsons'. Whether this was from their long association with the naval port of Portsmouth or from their one-eyed appearance when viewed head-on I cannot say – their route-indicator stencil-frames were carried on the lefthand of the corridor connection when seen from that angle, while the motorman's window was on the opposite side with access through the luggage compartment behind. No other prewar electric multiple-unit stock could offer corridor connections between sets, so their route-indicators were fitted centrally on the end of each driving motor-coach or trailer in the same way as suburban units. Sixteen months later, electric services from Victoria to Portsmouth were inaugurated using similar stock, but in this case one four-car set was detached from the main buffet car portion for Bognor Regis at Barnham Junction, with a corresponding link-up in the reverse direction.

There were plans afoot for further extensions to the third-rail network, but only the coastal line east from Chichester was completed before war threatened a second time. Local trains to Brighton were formed of pairs of 2-BIL or 2-HAL sets, while stopping services over the Portsmouth Direct line were similarly provided for. Maunsell's coach design was excellent for the period, giving a major improvement over generations of non-corridor steam stock, although corridor facilities on two-coach sets were limited to individual carriages. It is worth noting that this 'internal corridor' arrangement was copied in certain varieties of BR Standard stock 20 years later. . . . Whilst in no way belittling the great strides made since in bogie-design and quality of trackwork, it is indisputable that Maunsell's main-line electrified stock gave a high standard of reliability and comfort for more than 30 years, with nothing more than a change of livery to show for it.

38

Left: The inaugural electric train to Portsmouth, bearing a special facsimile of the City's Coat of Arms on its corridor connection, consisted of 4-RES set 3058. It was seen off from Waterloo on 8 March 1937 by a distinguished group but, sadly, this particular unit did not survive World War II. /*The News, Portsmouth*

Below: For more than 30 years Maunsell's 2-BIL electric sets were a familiar sight on stopping services to Portsmouth. Unit No 2030 leaves Liss for the coast on 5 July 1969./*Author*

8
New Poles For Old

It was generally agreed in Portsmouth that something must be done about the trams. With the majority of them approaching 30 years old, a handful even older, and with tracks dating back in one instance to 1865 it seemed high time to consider what was best to be done. Ben Hall, who had taken over the twin position of Manager and Engineer from Mr Spaven and Mr Lironi respectively in 1926, was very much alive to the problems of an ageing tramway and set about making improvements within the constraints imposed upon him. A number of trams were refurbished internally as they came due for overhaul and a new, brighter livery of scarlet and white began to replace the older crimson lake and cream. The original shade may be seen on the preserved tram No 84, of which more in a later chapter. In one last bid to save the trams, a new design by Mr Hall was approved and built in North End depot during 1930. It had several novel features, though it was not possible to depart from the four-wheel design of previous cars in view of limited clearances in some streets. It was fitted with air brakes, a cantilever truck and domed roof yet, despite its advanced design and

Right: Ben Hall's tramcar (No 1) under construction at North End depot in October 1930. The Peckham cantilever truck can be seen on the traverser.
/Portsmouth City Archivist

attractive appearance, it was destined to be the sole example of its kind, taking over the evocative number 1 and sporting the new livery. With a fleet of over a hundred tramcars, any decision as to their future was bound to have far reaching effects. And so it proved. . . .

Soon after the trials with Ben Hall's new No 1 car, the Corporation took the decision to abandon trams gradually in favour of trolley and motor buses. Readers will recall that Gosport had replaced its tramway system at the end of 1929, but Portsmouth wanted to retain the cleanliness of electric traction. Furthermore, with a quantity of poles already in position and much expertise in connection with overhead wires, it seemed a logical step. By 1933 tenders were out for the supply of 15 assorted types of trolley vehicle, to determine which might be best suited to Portsmouth's particular needs. Two main bodybuilders were selected; Metro-Cammell were chosen to build four and English Electric the remaining eleven. Four manufacturers produced the chassis with assorted combinations of control gear and there was one three-axle version from each of Leyland, AEC, Karrier and Sunbeam. The 60-seater six-wheelers were a trifle surprising in view of some sharp corners

Top: A line-up of Portsmouth's older trams in Goldsmith Avenue, waiting for football fans to leave Fratton Park in the early 1930s./*The News, Portsmouth*

Above: High Street, Old Portsmouth, showing interlaced tram tracks in a narrow part. /*The News, Portsmouth*

Right: Former Southampton 'Toastrack' tramcar, which became No 104 in the Portsmouth fleet, fitted with boat-shaped superstructure and illuminated for the Silver Jubilee of King George V and Queen Mary in 1935. /*The News, Portsmouth*

Above: With the tram tracks removed from Portsbridge, service 3 has become the preserve of trolleys. AEC No 21 approaches Hilsea on a southbound journey to Fawcett Road and South Parade Pier while one of the first series is completing the circular route back to Cosham, followed by petrol-engined TSM No 84 on service A. All three buses feature English Electric bodywork in this 1936 view./*The News, Portsmouth*

and limited clearances – all those factors that had constrained the tramcars to a four-wheeled truck instead of bogies – and it was said that the last trolley from this group, being taller than the rest, was responsible for there being further excavations outside Portsmouth & Southsea station, to give sufficient headroom under the High Level platforms. Another important consideration making possible the inauguration of trolleys in the City was the provision of a new depot and workshop in Highland Road, Eastney, in 1932. The first trolley buses began running in August 1934 on an experimental route between Cosham Railway Gates and South Parade Pier via North End, Fratton Road and Fawcett Road. Trams ceased to operate on service 3 and 4, these routes being taken over by the new trackless vehicles.

Perhaps this is a good point to mention about the rather quaint system of route numbering that existed in Portsmouth since the early days of trams right up to the present time, in one form or another.

Whether of letters or numbers, routes have generally been designated by adjacent characters, say A-B, for out-and-back journeys to be distinguished from one another. This became more logical when routes were extended to form circular services. Tram services were originally given letters but, from 1927, these were changed to numerals while the newly developed motor bus routes were designated by letters. With the arrival of trolleys, they were also given route numbers as they steadily displaced their tracked predecessors. This dual system of numbers and letters survived till the 1960s, route letters for motor buses being phased out to coincide with final abandonment of the trolleys in 1963. As services became more complicated, suffix letters were sometimes added – eg 1A, 2A – but this was never applied to the experimental 15 trolleys since their destination screens (like so much else about them) were non-standard; they were never altered throughout their career.

Experiences in service led the Transport Department to decide to standardise on the AEC chassis with English Electric equipment for future trolley buses. A further nine two-axle vehicles were ordered, with a new design of English Electric bodywork quite different from previous examples in the Corporation fleet. None of the first 24 vehicles carried

Left: Away from the main roads and tram tracks, conditions could be hazardous! Madeira Road, Portsmouth, in the winter of 1930, seems to be causing difficulties with its muddy 'surface'.
/*The News, Portsmouth*

Below: Last days for the 'green trams'. Two ex-Gosport cars can be seen in this glimpse of Cowplain depot, those with reversed staircases being original Light Railway stock. Former steam tram 'Lifu' was used as a store outside, still showing traces of its ship-yard ancestry./*Mr & Mrs Leitch*

batteries, a feature that affected their usefulness during World War II and one which was not repeated on future orders. With this nucleus of trackless electric vehicles, trams had ceased to run northwards beyond North End from 1 October 1934. This called into question the whole future of the green cars of the Portsdown & Horndean Light Railway, which continued to provide its regular services between Horndean and South Parade Pier as though nothing was happening. In view of future plans for expansion of the trolley network, the Corporation now wished to sever the tracks north of the depot at North End, which would have isolated the green trams and caused a reversion to their position pre-1924. With the Gosport system converted to motor buses and no route open to them south of Cosham nor west to Fareham, the Horndean system was offered for sale. As the Corporation did not want it – their future being pinned upon a combination of motor and trolley buses – the last Provincial tramway was purchased by Southdown

Motor Services Ltd and closed down after the final tram on 9 January 1935. Meanwhile, within the City, the rundown of Corporation trams was proceeding much quicker than expected: the Ben Hall car was sold to Sunderland, where it ran in modified form until 1953, while further orders for no less than 76 AEC trolley buses were placed! While retaining English Electric control gear, bodywork was to be built by Craven – who also won an order to build the bodies for 30 Leyland motor buses concurrently.

The final act in this saga of Portsmouth's tramways was played out on 10 November 1936, when the last cars made their sentimental journey to the depot. Thereafter only one urban tramway survived in Hampshire – operated by Southampton Corporation – which I shall deal with in a later chapter. Only one of Pompey's trams was retained, being a former horse-drawn car (No 84) which will be mentioned again in the concluding part of this volume. Otherwise, the City of Portsmouth lost a distinctive sound overnight for, within the span of two years, both electric systems that had served its people for more than three decades had come to an end. Of course, all trace did not disappear overnight: many

Above left: Purbrook in 1933, with Southdown Leyland Titan TD1 No 913 (UF 7413) heading south on service 41 to Fratton Bridge and South Parade Pier. Using highbridge covered-top double-deck buses on this ex-Southsea Tourist route alongside elderly open-top trams must have been crucial in competition for passengers./*The News, Portsmouth*

Left: As car No 6 enters Cowplain depot after its final run from Cosham, the solemn faces tell their own tale. /*C. H. T. Marshall*

Above: Like a scene from a Keystone Cops film Cosham's Fire Brigade hurtles along the disused tram lines at North End with a Ford 'T' appliance in 1935. /*The News, Portsmouth*

Right: Epitomising the image of Portsmouth in the 1930s – a magical scene captured by the illuminated Guildhall on 30 November 1934. /*The News, Portsmouth*

City streets retained their cobbles and embedded iron rails, while at Cosham the girder bridges of the Light Railway remained as a stark reminder. At the time of writing there is the quiet backwater of Rugby Road which has been left unspoiled, with cobble-setts and interlaced track as mute testimony to our forefathers and their 'people's carriage'.

9
At the Rainbow's End

Though I am an unashamed admirer of land-based vehicles, whether on road or rail, it would be churlish to dismiss out-of-hand those other forms of transportation upon which the British – as an island race – must now rely when we run out of terra firma. In this chapter I should like to take a look at our traditional seaborne traffic through the Solent, at those quaint tethered floating bridges and briefly at the new technological wonder, aircraft.

Having two major ports within 20 miles of each other along the Hampshire coast, in addition to innumerable smaller harbours, havens and estuaries that abound between Bosham and Lymington, the whole Solent area inland for a score of miles or more is very dependant upon the sea. No one who has stood beside a main road on a fine summer weekend could be left in doubt of the tremendous attraction of this whole coastline both for day visitors and holidaymakers intent on some further destination. Was it not the *raison d'etre* for the Landport and Southsea Tramway in the 1860s, to provide transport to Clarence Pier? What of the ill-fated Langston to St Helens train ferry? And was not Southampton the gateway to Africa or the New World? For centuries, foes and traders from abroad had aimed to gain a foothold along this coast, which has many bastions

still standing to recall their twin endeavours, both military and mercenary. Southampton thrived upon its merchant shipping as Portsmouth did upon its Naval Dockyard, each playing host to sea-going giants that have earned their places in history. Yet smaller ports like Emsworth, Gosport, Fareham, Hamble and Lymington have all played a part while an armada of small craft is moored at Langston, Portchester, Bursledon and Buckler's Hard with more across the Solent at Bembridge and at Cowes. This magnetic effect of waterways is not, perhaps, so remarkable when one remembers that (apart from Wight) both Portsea and Hayling are islands!

The docks at Southampton featured in the development of the railway from its earliest days. The 'Old Docks' had been established long before the half century covered in this book, while the Western or 'New Docks' were developed between the wars on reclaimed land between the Royal Pier and Millbrook. In addition, Red Funnel steamers ply between the Royal Pier and Cowes, with small launches providing a link across Southampton Water from the Town Quay to Hythe Pier. In the days before the Great War a local passenger train

Left: Fareham Creek, by the viaduct, in 1936.
/*The News, Portsmouth*

Above: Drewry 204hp diesel shunter D2291 causes havoc to road traffic while shunting Southampton Town Quay on 6 February 1967./*Author.*

Right: Cameo scene on the Town Quay, Southampton, as Drummond's C14 0—4—0T 77s simmers in the winter sunshine between duties on 31 January 1959./*Author*

had acted as go-between from Southampton Terminus along Platform Road – past the South Western Hotel – to both the Town Quay and Royal Pier, using steam Railmotors not unlike those built for the Fratton-East Southsea line in 1903; however, as with the Southsea branch and the line to Stokes Bay, passenger traffic ceased with hostilities. On all three routes it was never resumed, but at least in the case of the Town Quay some freight facilities survived until 1967. No longer would wagons trundle across Canute Road into Platform Road, being diverted instead through either Eastern or Western Docks, to be shunted on Town Quay by a diminutive survivor of the Railmotor period converted to an 0-4-0T since being severed from its carriage. The tracks themselves were not wholly abandoned but, terminated by buffer-stops practically opposite the South Western Hotel, they lingered on as a sidings till the first small 204hp Drewry diesel-shunter finally ousted Drummond's last little C14 Motor-tank, 77s.

Following early rivalry with the Great Western, both the South Western and its successor, the Southern Railway, did not seriously consider the Weymouth route for Channel Islands traffic. Theirs was handled

Above: The Royal Yacht *Victoria and Albert* entering King George V Graving Dock, Southampton, in 1933./*The News, Portsmouth*

Left: Cunard liner *Queen Mary* at the berth subsequently known as the Ocean Terminal, Southampton Docks. /*The News, Portsmouth*

Right: Rebuilt Bulleid 'West Country' 4–6–2 No 34095 *Brentor* slowly guides 'The Statesman' boat train towards the Canute Road exit from Southampton Docks on 14 April 1962./*Author*

through Southampton, perpetuating a duality of approach that was not finally solved until the 1960s, when the Western Region gave up their interest at Weymouth in exchange for the Southern's empire west of Salisbury. This enabled all services for Jersey and Guernsey to be concentrated on Weymouth but worked from Waterloo by the Southern, leaving Southampton free to indulge in international passenger traffic and, following its decline, in containers. It is apocalyptic that steam railways and giant passenger liners – the legendary Cunard 'Queens' and Union Castle ships in particular – should have both ebbed out of fashion together. . . .

If boat trains at Southampton meant the very best that the railway could muster, including Pullmans for some ocean liner expresses, at Lymington on summer Saturdays they were something else again! They were an institution that survived until September 1966, after which electrification of the Waterloo-Southampton-Bournemouth line and its adjoining branch from Brockenhurst to Lymington Pier made such weekly junketings in the peak season rather unnecessary. Of course, before the days of almost universal car-suffrage, it was not difficult to see why the Southern had capitalised on the popularity of the Isle of Wight as a holiday resort; no matter whether passengers travelled down by way of Portsmouth or Lymington, both the ferries that took them across the Solent and the little trains that met them on arrival were all under the same benign management at Waterloo. There will be a more detailed account of summer Saturday traffic in a subsequent chapter; suffice it to say for the present that Lymington boat trains were always worth a second glance. Their motive power was seldom equal to that provided for Southampton Docks, owing to the inadequacies of the turntable at Brockenhurst, where the train-engine from Waterloo gave way to something rather smaller yet capable of handling 10 well-loaded corridors over the 5¼-mile branch to the mouth of the Lymington river. On its best form, the observer might find that Nine Elms had rostered a doughty D15 4-4-0 (or a 'Schools' in the final years of steam) for the gallop down the main to Brockenhurst, while a chirpy '700' or Q 0-6-0 could manage 350 tons well enough amid the open heath and verdant woodland that comprises much of the New Forest along its coastal strip. The distinctive three-disc steam locomotive headcode for this train was lost after 1965

Above: Lymington Pier – Waterloo boat trains on summer Saturdays were regularly powered by 0–6–0s as far as Brockenhurst. On 23 July 1960 Q class No 30541 was in charge of the 1.28pm train, awaiting passengers from the Car Ferry *Freshwater./Author*

Left: With Royal Train headcode exhibited, T9 4–4–0 No 729 steams away from South Railway Jetty with Pullman coaches carrying HRH The Prince of Wales from Portsmouth Dockyard back to London after the naming ceremony of HMS *Duke of Gloucester* in 1935.
/The News, Portsmouth

Top right: Imperial Airways Flying Boat *Courtier* at Vickers Supermarine factory in the Isle of Wight.
/The News, Portsmouth

Bottom right: Schneider Cup Air Races brought large crowds to Southsea beaches. The Italian team pose with their entry near the Round Tower.
/The News, Portsmouth

for, with the removal of Brockenhurst's turntable in preparation for electrification, it was necessary to use an ambidextrous diesel for its final season.

On the Portsmouth line until 1937 a large proportion of trains were handled by 4-4-0s, with a handful of new 'Schools' engines being the star performers. Three-cylinder U1 2-6-0s made a less spectacular contribution while the seven N15x 'Remembrance' engines – newly converted from 'Baltic' tanks to 4-6-0s – were also to be found over this difficult road. On the sweeping curve of the short branch to South Railway Jetty, not used for regular traffic but often as a siding for surplus carriage stock, the infrequent passage of a Royal Train would presage nothing larger than a 'Greyhound' 4-4-0 over its Victorian timbers, perhaps at the head of a handsome

rake of Pullmans to welcome some foreign potentate. With the coming of war in 1939 it had short shrift, being so close to possible naval targets, and few pictures of it seem to survive showing anything other than stored carriages. But for those fortunate enough to visit the South Railway Jetty, there is still an air about the place that is entirely in keeping with its century-old past, where soldiers and sailors and great men trod when Britain was in the 'first division' among world states.

While much of the blame for the railway's decline can be levelled at the internal-combustion engine that transformed our roads, since the 1920s a new and powerful force had been emerging to decimate international passenger shipping, if not the whole of mercantile marine – the development of aviation. And if I am personally almost wholly ignorant of the intricacies of aircraft, no one can be unaware of their effect on trans-Atlantic travel or even on humbler traffic to Europe, the Channel Islands or the Isle of Wight! In the 1930s two modest airports were established within the mainland Solent area, at Portsmouth and at Eastleigh, while another came into being at Hurn with counterparts on the Isle of Wight, Jersey and Guernsey. Major international airports at Heathrow and Gatwick have developed since World War II but, earlier, there had been scope for Imperial Airways flying-boats out of Southampton and their attendant trains from Waterloo. It goes without saying that Naval and Royal Air Force bases in the area continue to maintain an airborne capability, while the last 15 years have seen the emergence of new technological wonders in the shape of hovercraft and hydrofoil. Both are now in passenger service between the mainland and the Isle of Wight, a development that has militated against new investment in next-generation conventional ferries – Sealink's long established Portsmouth - Ryde service is currently maintained by just three turbine-driven ships now 30 years old. Sadly, British Rail pensioned-off their last paddle-steamers a decade ago. However,

Top: Car Ferry *Wootton* and PS *Ryde* are framed against Gosport's naval background, with HMS *Dolphin* submarine base clearly visible on 25 July 1961. */Author*

Above: Clarence Pier between the wars, with two Southern Railway paddle steamers tied up alongside. */The News, Portsmouth*

despite the inroads caused by car ownership on conventional passenger vessels, there has been a marked upsurge in roll-on roll-off traffic using car ferries across the Solent and further afield to Europe. From the slipway in Old Portsmouth to Wootton Creek at Fishbourne or between Lymington Pier and Yarmouth the vehicular ferries of British Rail serving the Isle of Wight are almost always busy and, in summer at weekends, prior booking must be made months in advance. An increase in the capacity of the ferries merely allows more vehicles to be transhipped, so the problem is not likely to be resolved – in spite of fairly formidable charges for vehicles. On the Lymington-Yarmouth route the car ferries handle all traffic, whether vehicular or not, whereas from Portsmouth the traffic is split. While car ferries always operate direct between Wootton Creek and Old Portsmouth – now Broad Street slipway – all other passengers

normally sail from Portsmouth Harbour to Ryde Pier Head, with some services still calling at Clarence Pier in summer. No large vessels now call at South Parade Pier since the most recent fire, though both Red Funnel and Southern (British Railways shipping services are now known universally as Sealink) ships formerly used it in the summer season.

There are a number of purely local waterborne services that should be mentioned before leaving this subject, which might justify a whole volume all to itself for those fascinated by shipping or aviation. A small launch plies between Eastney and Hayling Island, but a shadow of the once grandiose scheme for a railway extension from Fratton that would have linked Eastney, Hayling, Langston and Havant in a circular route – in recent years the Hayling Ferry has been taken over by the City of Portsmouth. Another more important and prosperous ferry operates between Portsmouth Harbour and Gosport Hard for passengers and cycles. Two companies, based one on each side of the Harbour, formerly worked the service jointly; they have since amalgamated to form the Portsmouth Harbour Ferry Company. Another local ferry operates between Southampton Town Quay and Hythe Pier

Left: The old booking office for Harbour launches, on the Gosport side. A 1934 Provincial bus No 27 (CG 9612) waits for passengers on the Park Road service./*The News, Portsmouth*

Below: Varos and *Ferry Princess* are kept busy with passengers at the Portsmouth Harbour pontoon. Beyond may be seen two Southern Railway paddle steamers, while empty carriage stock was often stored on the branch line from Portsmouth Harbour station to South Railway Jetty.
/*The News, Portsmouth*

Bottom: A wartime perspective of the Floating Bridge *Alexandra* — the lorries were returning from dumping rubble from war-damage on beaches near Stokes Bay. It was often open on one side only in its later years.
/*The News, Portsmouth*

across Southampton Water, having been formally established in 1874. The present 700 yard Pier was opened in 1880 but, since 1922, has been served by a unique 2ft gauge railway electrified on the third-rail system with a pair of four-wheeled locomotives and several carriages and wagons. Track is single throughout and only one train-set is in use at any time, the locomotive being coupled at the landward end, being driven from a trailer coach when propelling towards the Pier Head. Both Ferry and Pier Railway are owned by the General Estates Company Ltd, controlled from offices at Hotspur House in Hythe. Unlike the launches on the Portsmouth Harbour service, which have had such divers names as *Varos, Vadne, Vita* and *Ferry Princess* (to name but a few!), all Hythe ferries purchased new since 1927 have rejoiced in the name *Hotspur* by virtue of a connection with the Welsh Percy family. The Hythe Pier Railway is the only public narrow-gauge system presently providing a service within the Solent area throughout the year.

Finally, one cannot forget the various floating bridges. All but one have now ceased in the Solent area, but there were formerly two more in use during the period covered by this book. At Cowes one plies across the

Medina river between East and West Cowes, this facility being also offered by Red Funnel steamers as part of their service from Southampton Royal Pier. A veritable antique survived across Portsmouth Harbour between Point, Old Portsmouth and a slipway adjacent to the launches' Pontoon at Gosport until 1959. Throughout World War II two vessels – the *Duke of York* and the *Alexandra* – provided the service alternately, to allow for regular maintenance, but in later years only the latter could be maintained and that became increasingly fitful and spasmodic. To judge from the ever increasing congestion that now exists all along the Gosport-Fareham road and at interchanges from the M27 and M275 motorways at Fareham and Portsmouth respectively, that old chain-operated car ferry is sadly missed! A splendidly-evocative

recording of it is available on an LP record from Argo, 'Sounds of Bygone Transport'. Last of all, across the Itchen at Southampton could be found a pair bridging the gap between Woolston and Southampton, with normally simultaneous departures from either side. A third bridge was kept in reserve to cover repairs, since there was practically a 24-hour service in operation. Privately owned until 1934, the Itchen Floating Bridges were acquired by Southampton Corporation and remained in operation until a new road bridge opened in 1977. An attractive and well-illustrated booklet is available to document their rise and fall in greater detail, obtainable from the Museum in Southampton.

If motorways and the development of road transport vehicles have changed the face of the Solent area more than our grandparents could ever have imagined, at least in the last decade there has come about a realisation that all forms of transport are inter-related and often benefit mutually by closer liaison rather than any particular form gaining some temporary unfair advantage to the detriment, ultimately, of all. British Railways took the opportunity, when electrifying the Waterloo - Southampton - Bournemouth main line, to include a new station to cater for Southampton Airport (formerly Eastleigh airport, between Eastleigh and Swaythling). Various bus companies provide connecting links between ferry terminals and railway stations, in addition to their taking passengers to shopping centres and other popular venues. It has taken a long time for this change of attitude to develop and perhaps some of the credit may be apportioned to the oil sheikhs, whose sudden fourfold increase in the cost of crude in the early 1970s managed to focus official minds wonderfully!

Left: Itchen Floating Bridges 12 and 14 may be seen in this 1970s picture, even as the new structure destined to replace them is taking shape./*Author*

10
The Pursuit of Excellence

We have seen in a previous chapter how the larger bus companies became established after World War I. The very business of operating stage-carriage services profitably and without losing ground to the host of small operators that were continually springing up was sufficient for their concentration – for the greater part – until the Road Traffic Act 1930 brought a much needed sense of order to the whole business of licensing bus routes. Once the dust had settled, there was scope for a thorough-going review of the whole field of road passenger transport, made all the more necessary because of the steady reduction in various tramway undertakings and the closures of some unprofitable branch railways. All the while railway companies were buying their way into major bus operators, both to 'hedge their bets' and to influence policy by encouraging inter-availability of tickets where services might otherwise conflict. Good examples of this may be seen in pre-Nationalisation railway timetables: in the Solent area this was almost exclusively the preserve of the Southern Railway. But other influences were also making their mark. . . .

When Southdown bought out Southsea Tourist in 1925 they gained more than a fleet of Dennis buses, for they took over an already thriving coach business. As other small operators decided to sell out to the giants, more routes and tours were acquired in addition to a multitude of assorted vehicles. An absorbing tale unfolds in the pages of the official *Southdown Story* and also in the History of Hants & Dorset Motor Services, as told by Colin Morris; even in the various fleet histories published by the PSV Circle and the Omnibus Society, the variety and numbers of acquired vehicles that flit in and out of the story as each year goes by provide an insight into the empire-building that took place with almost monotonous regularity. A comparative few of the acquired vehicles stayed with their new owners for more than a season; most were promptly resold to a new generation of minor operators or to dealers – and since disappeared without trace. World War II put paid to the rest, as well as siphoning-off the cream of petrol-engined coaches for war service. A few sepia postcards and licensing authorities' records are the epitaph of practically all coaches between the wars, which makes it all the more difficult to grasp for those of us not fortunate enough to have experienced the situation at first hand. To one unable to recall beyond the mid-war years of 1943/4, the 1930s seem like a beautiful dream that has floated away, a headlong unreality of excellence.

Yet whatever had gone before, the year 1935 stands out as a watershed. Southdown purchased the Portsdown and Horndean Light Railway and promptly closed it down,

Above: A galaxy of Southdown's best coaches was provided for the PIMCO employees outing in 1933. Tilling-Stevens and Leyland Tiger vehicles typify the Company's pursuit of excellence. Wickham Square has change little in the intervening years./*The News, Portsmouth*

Centre right: The swing-arm petrol pumps of Bond's Garage and the overhead gas lamps portray Waterlooville in the 1930s, but the double-deck bus and recently-removed tram tracks serve to remind us how quickly the scene changed. /*C. H. T. Marshall*

Bottom right: F. G. Tanner's 'Denmead Queen' services were operated by several handsome Wadham-bodied Thornycroft buses. This CD model, RV 1844, became No 547 in Southdown's fleet in 1935. /*C. H. T. Marshall*

the last tram squealing into the Cowplain depot near midnight on 9 January. Within weeks the overhead was cut down and the tracks lifted; *requiescat in pace*. Not long after, Mr Tanner's 'Denmead Queen' business was taken over together with its routes to Hambledon, so that Southdown's mastery beyond Portsdown Hill was undisputed. A trio of Denmead Queen Thornycroft buses remained in service with Southdown until the war – a rare accolade, in view of their increasing standardisation on Leyland vehicles.

At Hoeford, after the demise of the trams, there was something of a vacuum. Some small six-wheeled Chevrolets were bought new and, when it was found impracticable to maintain services adequately, Gosport & Fareham Omnibus Company was forced to hire from neighbouring operators or see its routes taken over by a determined group of smaller firms ready and eager to make the most of it. Half a dozen former charabancs, that Southdown had sent for rebodying to Short Brothers in 1928 as open-top double-deckers came in very useful. They were a mixture of N and G7 chassis and all were subsequently purchased, together with a handful of Leyland Lion PLSC single-deckers from Hants & Dorset. Fortified with these fairly primitive vehicles, eight new AEC coaches with Harrington bodywork joined the fleet in 1934, to be followed by a steady stream of corresponding 'Regent' double-deckers with highbridge Park Royal bodies commencing in 1936. Just as Southdown was aiming to standardise on products from Lancashire, so Provincial set its seal of approval on those from Southall.

Hants & Dorset achieved their 'coup' with a spectacular double in 1935, first with their acquisition of the excursions and tours side of Elliott Brothers' 'Royal Blue' coach business based in Bournemouth, then followed the purchase of Ransom's 'Tourist' fleet centred on Southampton. Express services and a proportion of the rolling-stock were transferred to the Tilling Company's Western and Southern

Top: While Hayling services demanded single-deckers – like this Tilling-Stevens B39A6 model, with Short Bros body (716; ACD 116) – petrol-engined double-deckers could operate on most other routes from Portsmouth. Both vehicles were to be found at South Parade Pier in the mid-1930s./ *Surfleet (D. Clark)*

Above: The roof luggage compartment was a feature of Royal Blue coaches for 20 years. Car 3104, an early Leyland Tiger TS2, depicts the attractive livery and style that made Royal Blue Express services respected throughout the south./ *A. B. Cross*

National subsidiaries in the west of England, who continued to use 'Royal Blue' as the title for all their express services thereafter. Hants & Dorset built upon the existing excursions and tours side of both its new acquisitions, even retaining their old

Above: Painted in the former Elliott Bros Royal Blue livery when new in 1936, Hants & Dorset Leyland Tiger TS7 F 574 (CEL 234) was repainted after one season in an attractive green and cream style thereafter. The distinctive Beadle coachwork and 7.6 litre petrol engine made this a superb vehicle for extended tours; it was renumbered 632 for one season in 1950, before disposal./*N. Hamshere*

liveries and fleet-titles for two seasons before absorbing the whole lot under its own name and livery to avoid possible confusion with 'Royal Blue' express coaches. From 1937 all Hants & Dorset coaches were painted green and cream, in a particularly attractive style that continued practically unchanged until the first postwar full-fronted vehicles appeared in 1951.

During the final years of the 1930s, Britain witnessed some of the finest workmanship and aesthetic design ever achieved in its transport history. In the Solent area this manifested itself in the superb Harrington-built coachwork for most of Southdown's Leyland Tigers, while Hants & Dorset preferred the Dartford firm of Beadle for their handsome vehicles. Indeed, some of the older coaches were rebodied by Beadle using the same styling, with distinctive streamlined hinged panel over the nearside front wing. For Hayling Island services, both stage-carriage and express, Southdown experienced a special problem owing to the restrictions imposed by the timber toll bridge linking Langston with North Hayling – to keep vehicle weight to within the permitted figure, all services were operated by single- deckers. When the older Tilling-Stevens vehicles became due for retirement, they were replaced by two series of Leyland 'Cub' buses with Park Royal bodies and eleven superior 'Cheetah' coaches. All these were retained for Hayling duties until the aged bridge was finally replaced by a modern structure devoid of restrictions in 1956. Though oil-engined vehicles were beginning to be ordered in increasing numbers, most larger companies and practically all the smaller ones continued to specify petrol engines for coaches until the war, both for quicker acceleration and quieter operation. In some instances the choice of a petrol engine might be made on the grounds of quietness, but it would be a fastidious customer who could find fault with the 8.6 litre six-cylinder diesel option offered by Leyland on their Tiger chassis during the period under review! Both Southdown and Hants & Dorset ordered oil-engined coaches for

Left: Calm before the storm (1): A peaceful scene at Gosport's historic railway station. Stroudley D1 0–4–2T No 2239 waits to depart with a train to Fareham./*Lens of Sutton*

Below left: Calm before the storm (2): One of the last petrol-engined double-deckers to be delivered to Portsmouth Corporation was TSM E60A6 No 80 (RV 1143), with 50-seat English Electric bodywork. /*Portsmouth City Archivist*

Bottom left: Calm before the storm (3): Old Chesil Rectory Tea House in Winchester, adjoining the GWR railway station. /*The News, Portsmouth*

Below: Calm before the storm (4): One of Hants & Dorset's first low-bridge buses with open staircases is dwarfed by the tower at Lee-on-the-Solent. /*R. Brown collection*

their final prewar touring season, which was just as well in the circumstances for many petrol-engined coaches were requisitioned by the Ministry of Defence for use in the war effort. Some were adapted as ambulances which, if not bombed during the war, survived to be re-united with their former operators when peace returned. Those pressed into active service were mostly lost beyond recall, as will be seen when we look at the war period and its aftermath in detail in Epoch III.

After the famous Munich episode in 1938, when a scrap of paper granted Britain one last summer of traditional pleasure after the false alarums and unpublished crisis-measures that had been circulating, it was like the calm before the storm. As in Beethoven's 'Pastoral Symphony', the suddenness of events in September 1939 came like a clap of thunder heralding menace after the summer heat; nothing would ever be quite the same again.

Top: Calm before the storm (5): Rivalling London or Glasgow in the number of its trams to be seen at any one time, Southampton's Above Bar thoroughfare was noted for the number and variety of its stores. /*Southern Newspapers Ltd*

Above: Calm before the storm (6): Before the lights went out all over Europe, Portsmouth AEC trolley bus No 204 (RV 4652) was illuminated for the Coronation in 1937 — carrying on the tradition begun with the trams. /*Portsmouth City Archivist*

Epoch III

1939-1949, Austerity and Hard Times

11
Evacuation and the Phoney War?

Once war was declared between Britain and Germany there was much activity to prepare, albeit belatedly, for what was to come. With the whole coastline at risk both from bombardment and invasion, it was natural that civic leaders should think of those least able to help themselves and arrange for those who wished to be evacuated into the countryside, away from obvious military targets. Some went from Clarence Pier across to the Isle of Wight by paddle-steamer; others boarded trains for Bournemouth and Petersfield while a remarkable array – to our eyes, 40 years on – of Portsmouth Corporation buses bustled about in all directions collecting, delivering and generally conveying young and old from their familiar homes to safer places 'out of town'. A unique collection of photographs of this first taste of the exigencies of war, evacuation, survives in the archives of Portsmouth's local newspaper *The News,* by whose kindness and generosity I am able to include a selection in this volume. One is struck by the orderliness of it all: the archetypal policeman showing the way, the spotless Corporation buses – Tilling-Stevens,

Left: Islands like Portsea and Hayling were especially vulnerable to attack by air and sea from an invader. In this aerial picture of Langstone Harbour both road and rail bridges connecting Hayling to the mainland can be seen, with a Southdown bus travelling northward to Havant.
/*The News, Portsmouth*

Above and right: Evacuation, Portsmouth style. Dozens of Corporation double-deck buses were mobilised to take children away from the most vulnerable areas at the beginning of the war./*The News, Portsmouth*

Crossley, Leyland – with their white roofs and ornate lining-out, more in keeping with Oktoberfest than Blitzkrieg. As one comes to examine later pictures of the war and its aftermath, the contrast is striking! But among the faces of the people there is no sign of panic or fear; later, after heavy bombing raids had taken their toll of lives and property, a sort of grim determination and wry humour is apparent – a microcosm of Britain under extreme pressure.

As 1939 slipped away the storm was gathering across the English Channel; at home, 1940 brought with it snow and ice to an extent that even the sea froze. Portsdown Hill became an ice-rink for vehicles while bus services from outlying villages and towns terminated at 'The George'. The pictures show, for the first time, bus roofs painted over from their familiar white or cream to grey or, in the case of some Southdown and Hants & Dorset vehicles, green. As winter melted into spring still there was no obvious indication of war, although bus and train services had been reduced and fuel rationing boosted the use of trolley buses. Then, at the end of May 1940, came Dunkirk – a remarkable exploit in which many small vessels from the Solent

Above: Outside 'The George', Southdown buses are forced to terminate short of their destination due to icy roads during the winter of 1940. Three Park Royal bodied Leyland TD5s appear in this picture, of which 206 and 208 have had South Parade Pier painted out on their blinds due to wartime restrictions.
/The News, Portsmouth

Above right: With bayonets fixed, soldiers stop Southdown Leyland TD3 No 971 at a road-block. Owing to wartime press censorship the bus' destination has been blanked out on the photograph, but it is probable it was near Fareham./*The News, Portsmouth*

area took part in bringing back men from the French and Belgian coast. In less than two months the war was on in earnest, with the first raid on Portsmouth taking place in daylight on 11 July 1940. The Battle of Britain had begun.

In an odd sort of way the commencement of actual hostilities and the involvement of the civilian population in 'front line' warfare may have made things easier to cope with. At least the 10 months of 'phoney war' was ended and it was possible to get some measure of the enemy's tactics. Black-out precautions, training of the 'Dads' Army' and unpredictable closures of roads or railway lines due to bombs – unexploded or otherwise – were to become the order of the

day, together with food rationing, an end to private motoring, no transport after nine o'clock at night, double summer-time to aid the farmers, 'utility' clothing standards and the terminaton of all luxuries as sweeteners. Winston S. Churchill had become Prime Minister 'for the duration' and, somewhere up in the blue sky above, our incredible Royal Air Force was knocking hell out of German fighters and bombers against all the odds. By October there was a lull in the bombing and the first round had been won by the defenders.

But if 1940 had been tough, the going was to get much rougher before it became easier again. Agreement was reached between the various bus companies to enable vehicles and crews to be out-stationed at night in less vulnerable districts, so far as possible. Corporation motor buses might be seen climbing Portsdown Hill at the end of the day, like the first electric trams 40 years earlier, to avoid losses from night bombing by the German Air Force, but the trolleys had to stay and take their chance. All one hundred had been renumbered in 1938 by the addition of 200 to the fleet numbers to avoid confusion with their motor bus counterparts. The experimental 15, together with the subsequent

nine AEC's with English Electric bodywork, were taken out of service due to timetable reductions caused by the war and because, in the event of power failure, these trolley buses had no batteries and would be stranded. All four of the six-wheelers were hired in due course to Pontypridd UDC, where they stayed until hostilities ended. The remainder were stored in the open, to be gradually brought back into traffic as the course of the war became more certain.

In Southampton, too, crews were encouraged to take their buses out of the high risk area into the countryside at night. When one sees pictures of the damage inflicted near the docks, around the Bargate or near railway stations, there was clearly much wisdom in this action. However, it must have presented some difficulty for crews not familiar with rural roads at night, particularly on headlamps dimmed to candle power, with New Forest animals roaming freely! But in Southampton, as in Portsmouth, the vehicles most at risk were those restrained by their overhead wires (and, since they were trams, by their street tracks, being the last municipal tramway anywhere along the south coast); not for them a hurried diversion down some narrow side street to avoid falling debris or an unexploded bomb! But if Southampton's trams were vulnerable, they continued to provide a service wherever possible. Daubed over in grey, they presented a grim picture to those having to use them, grimly portraying the bulldog tenacity of their people who suffered – along with other major ports and military or strategic targets – a series of relentless raids reducing whole streets to rubble. Some sidings were provided for them under cover of trees at the Bassett end of The Avenue and only one tram was lost due to war damage.

The real crunch for the Solent came in 1941. On 10 January there was the most appalling holocaust in Portsmouth, engulfing the Guildhall and many of the City's shopping areas in addition to the Clarence Pier and the recently modernised Harbour station. Some evidence of the extent of the

Top right: Woolston station after an air raid.
/*Southern Newspapers Ltd*

Centre right: A Southampton Corporation domed-roof car approaches the junction for Floating Bridge by the ruins of Holy Rood church.
/*Southern Newspapers Ltd*

Below: Beyond the Admiralty Pier, dense smoke hides the ruin of Portsmouth Harbour station, following an air raid on 10 January 1941, while Gosport launches huddle against the pontoon. Beyond them, the spars of HMS *Victory* can be seen stark against the sky.
/*The News, Portsmouth*

Above: One of Portsmouth's more striking long-lived buses, 1935 Leyland Titan TD4 No 130 (RV 6373) was still in almost original condition when photographed outside North End depot on 29 July 1959. Only four of this type were purchased by the Corporation./*Author*

destruction and devastation can be glimpsed from the local *News* pictures of the period, while planned demolition and clearance of unsafe structures called for a stream of lorries to carry away the rubble on the old floating bridge to Gosport, where it was used in due course to strengthen the beaches at Stokes Bay in preparation for D-Day. To make life even more difficult there was another cold spell, with vehicles again being unable to descend Portsdown Hill to the City. Then occurred an event which is the first that I am positively able to recall myself. On 4 March 1941 a massive bomb landed in the mud beside Portsbridge but failed to explode. Bomb disposal experts examined ways of dealing with it, while traffic was diverted either via Eastern Road – the fast new roadway built shortly before the war skirting the airport, linking

Milton with Farlington – or via Peronne Road and over an even newer bridge into the Highbury Estate at Cosham. This third bridge was not marked on German maps, having been built since the war across both Portcreek and the City's ancient Moat, involving a further breach of the ramparts after the manner of the railway, 90 years or so before. For one evening this narrow bridge carried virtually all the home-going traffic that normally travelled over Portsbridge; as a small child I watched in wonder as an endless stream of buses and cyclists made their way out of the City within a few yards of the family home at the eastern end of Military Road. One red Corporation bus especially caught my eye for, even in pre-school days, I was aware that they were not all the same. It was an important discovery for me . . . a double-deck bus of a kind with which Portsmouth was not over endowed – the all-Leyland Titan TD4 with V-fronted bodywork and destination displays similar to the 15 experimental trolley buses. Next day the bomb was defused and the regular pattern was resumed.

Within a week Portsmouth received another massive air attack, this time causing severe damage to Eastney depot. A number of motor buses suffered direct hits, including two of the 1939-series of oil-engined Leyland Cheetah single-deckers with Wadham bodywork. Some damage was also sustained by North End depot but no vehicles were lost there. With such savage attacks at night, our family and several of our neighbours took to sleeping in bunks in brick-lined storerooms under the old ramparts at the back of Military Road – since 1937 houses had been built only on the northern side of the road, the south side being still just a field. Though known colloquially as 'shelters', they were not purpose built as such but were part of the Ordnance fortifications from long ago. They were damp and stale-smelling, but each night several were filled with families who had no other form of protection. In the morning we would emerge from our nocturnal dormitories behind piles of sandbags to inspect the damage and prepare for the day. Once or twice after dark I was allowed to go to the doorway and join a little knot of silent people, recognised only by the dim glow of their cigarettes, to watch the aircraft overhead and see the sky lit up red from incendiary fires. Sometimes one could hear the whistle of bombs coming down, followed by the heavy crump of an explosion or the harsh chatter of ack-ack gunfire. When the 'all clear' siren sounded people drifted off to bed or went to make interminable cups of tea – it all seemed perfectly natural to me at the time!

Above: Part of Hilsea Lines fortification was removed in 1933 to build a new Southdown bus garage. During the war some of the storerooms under the old ramparts were used as air raid shelters./*The News, Portsmouth*

But while the populace faced up to the realities of war, by degrees the nation's resources were being adapted to cope with the new strains cast upon them. At Eastleigh in March 1941 took place the naming of O. V. S. Bulleid's first air-smoothed 4-6-2 locomotive No 21C1 *Channel Packet*, which was destined to revolutionise locomotive design and performance on the Southern until the very last breath of steam in July 1967. Twenty were to be built initially, with a further 10 following after the war at Nationalisation; because of their weight, the 'Merchant Navy' class (as they were called), were limited to main lines such as those from London to the Channel ports or from Waterloo to Bournemouth or Exeter. Apart from the striking appearance, Bulleid's design produced some technical innovations including chain-drive in an oil bath, Box-Pok wheels and boiler pressure of 280psi. Whilst some of these features were modified in due course as a result of several years' experience in traffic – the whole class was rebuilt with Walschaerts' valve gear and a more conventional appearance after removal of the air-smoothed casing from 1956 – yet some of the designer's unconventional brilliance

68

Top left: Wartime measures (1): Roadsigns were removed 'for the duration'.
/*The News, Portsmouth*

Centre left: Wartime measures (2): With blanked-out lamps, grey or dull paintwork, white wings and a 9pm curfew, Provincial buses also disguised destinations by using first letters only. In this 1942 view can be seen the restricted space of Fareham bus station, with Southdown TD3 No 971 (facing) and No 129 (rear), Hants & Dorset Bristol L5G No TS 809 and one of Gosport & Fareham's AEC Regents.
/*The News, Portsmouth*

Below left: Wartime measures (3): Old tram lines were removed from City streets to help the war effort.
/*The News, Portsmouth*

Below: Wartime measures (4): A Portsmouth Corporation lorry adapted to use methane gas. 'Heaven's Light our Guide!'
/*The News, Portsmouth*

Above: Wartime measures (5): After massive devastation in the City the scene from the Guildhall steps is like a concentration camp.
/*The News, Portsmouth*

Below: Wartime measures (6): Gas-masks for the girls, as they leave Portsmouth's Airspeed factory after work. The Crossley Condor bus at the front of the queue is the prototype No 74 (RV 720)./*The News, Portsmouth*

Bottom: First of a new breed – 21C1 *Channel Packet* at Eastleigh Works after the naming ceremony in 1941.
/*Southern Newspapers Ltd*

lingered with them into folklore; they were often credited with very fast running through the magic '100' barrier and a number of carefully documented exploits have passed down into history. As hostilities were drawing to a close in 1945 these giants begat a similar but lighter breed of steam engine that was to transform passenger traffic over a much wider area. We shall meet them a little later on.

For the time being the war effort was paramount and to meet it on the Southern a curious general purpose locomotive was put into service all over the south east, wherever the need was greatest. Of simple six-coupled design, the Q1 class had no frills but mustered great power for haulage of troop trains or munition specials and 40 were built during 1941 to help win the war. Numbered from C1 upwards and intended for a working life of 10 years, three were still active a quarter of a century later at the very eclipse of steam power. Despite an unsightly appearance, the Austerities earned the respect of many railwaymen and became affectionately known as 'Charlies' in later years. Certainly, when viewed from any angle, they presented a most unusual shape and again Box-Pok wheels were in evidence, quite alien to British tradition. Yet, when deftly handled to avoid slipping, these 0-6-0s were able to haul loads normally scheduled for S15 or 'King Arthur' 4-6-0 power but over lines

prohibited to such heavy engines – a valuable asset when main routes might be blocked by enemy action with vital supplies urgently needed.

As the war entered its third year, Britain's natural inventiveness began to fashion means for its survival until the military might of the United States could be ranged alongside to ensure ultimate victory.

Above: Bulleid's war-winner, the unconventional Q1 class. No 33020 backs through the bomb-damaged Gosport station on 21 May 1962, on a peaceful mission to the RN Victualling Yard./*Author*

Below: In war, as in peace, the marshalling yards at Eastleigh are always busy. S15 4–6–0 No 510 waits for a clear road as Z 0–8–0T No 952 comes past with a special freight./*The News, Portsmouth*

12
Gas Masks and School Satchels

For readers too young to have experienced the war, it would seem very strange to keep one ear open for the siren whilst sitting at a school desk. Essential equipment for a five-year old going to school in 1942 would include the traditional leather satchel, perhaps a sandwich or an apple for mid-morning and an oblong cardboard box. The box was not for games but, at the warning sound of an air-raid siren, would be opened and its curious contents worn by the child while stumbling in orderly haste to the shelter. The gas mask would be used in practice while the danger lasted, in case the enemy should drop canisters of poison-gas instead of the more familiar objects of destruction. Starting at such an early age we accepted these things (which are curios today) as part of the normal way of life without question. I cannot recall any child being depressed by them, though it was nice to be able to remove them and replace them in their cartons until another day, to be able to breathe freely again and savour the scent of fresh flowers in the garden. . . .

My first school was in a private house on the slopes of Portsdown Hill, appropriately enough in Southdown Road. It was run by a kind, matronly lady who provided a first introduction to the world of learning for upwards of 20 children between the ages of five and eight. School being more than a mile away from home at Hilsea, there were two ways of getting there and even more –

as I was to discover – of coming back. At first, beginning with the autumn term in 1942, I was accompanied to school on the bus; this was to be my initiation into the daily experience of public transport. The nearest bus-stop was at St Colman's Church, a request stop along the Havant Road beyond the 'Red Lion' at Cosham; from there it was then just a short walk up Widley Lane. An alternative route involved catching a bus halfway up Portsdown Hill to the other end of Widley Lane, with a pleasant ramble down if the weather was fine. My earliest recollections are of crowded, steamy double-deck buses lit by dim bulbs with a regular panic to get to the rear platform in time for the request stop, pushing through hordes of giant-like adults! Occasionally I was unlucky and the bus went past the stop as far as Drayton, which meant a tearful explanation to teacher on late arrival. It was also about this time, when travelling on the Southdown 31 service, that I noticed the 'lowbridge' phenomenon. Local buses to Farlington, Havant or Emsworth on services 31A or 31B did not seem to have this feature of sunken upper-deck gangway on the righthand side of the bus, but if I was to catch a 31 for Chichester or Bognor – faraway places to a five-year old – it always seemed to be chock-a-block and to have the low gangway.

After the dark, gloomy mornings of the

winter, there was a temptation to take an earlier bus up Portsdown Hill for a walk before school. Most days the bus would plod slowly up the steep hill from the junction at its foot, with my ear already tuned to the musical sounds of Leyland transmissions. Southdown's early diesels were ponderous and reliable, but a trifle frustrating to a child worried about being late for school! One morning, however, the 40B service for Drift Road offered a petrol-guzzling Titan TD1 open-top bus – temporarily shrouded in a hideous canvas-roof affair to enable it to be used for 365 days in the year, not just during summer – in place of the usual vehicle. At least, the diesel had gone on ahead and the elderly '800' Titan had some obscure duty as a relief – it was no surprise to find many extra buses running at peak times in those days – but my mother and I were more concerned about prompt arrival at Avalon School than the height of the platform step! Off went the old TD1, with evocative back-firing sounds from the exhaust as it coasted down from Cosham railway bridge to the Post Office, exuding an unmistakable whiff of 'pool' petrol fumes in the process. A brief pause, two wallops on the bell-push and there followed the classic sound of a petrol bus pulling away from rest. . . . Ahead was the oiler, preparing for a change down into second gear for the climb to Widley Lane, but the ancient greyhound stayed in third and prepared to do battle on the ascent. With little fear of other traffic trying to pass, third gear screaming abuse, the 'spirit of '29' pulled out and flew past its more modern rival, while one young passenger experienced his first thrill of speed. Can you wonder that, in the 1970s, one of my greatest pleasures has been to have an occasional ride on Southdown's preserved example No 813 (UF 4813)?

For the under-sixes school ended at lunchtime, when I would usually be met by one or other of my parents for the journey home. Generally it would be my mother, but sometimes it would be my father in his police uniform, riding his bicycle home

Below: Not designed for beauty or speed, the temporary canvas roofs fitted to Southdown's 1929 open-top Titans subtracted nothing from their quaintness – 823 (UF 4823) was based at Hilsea throughout World War II for schools and relief work. /*Southdown M.S. Ltd*

from an eight-hour shift on duty. He would cycle down Court Lane, with me on the cross-bar, until we came to Jacob's Ladder – the footbridge over the railway just east of Cosham station. Here we would hump the heavy bicycle up the steps before pausing to see if there was a train coming, for there was an excellent view of both platforms beyond the cattle-dock. Then, if no one appeared to be about near the houses of Highbury, I would climb up again on to the crossbar for the ride over the 'pipe' to Military Road. Within a year or two I was to spend many hours fishing for tiddlers from that concrete-covered tube, which allowed the tide to flow right round the island of Portsea beneath its newest (and shortest-lived) bridge. Built in 1940, it was to be demolished in 1968 when a new motorway complex for the M27 was being planned; its place has been taken by a footbridge.

By the summer of 1943 it was not always possible for someone to meet me from school. Without the present-day volume of traffic it was not too difficult for a child to cross the Havant Road, with the prospect of a pleasant dawdle along the way home, but one day I stood at the bus-stop alone and waited. . . . At about twelve-thirty a bus was due that did not run all the way into Portsmouth from Havant; sometimes (I discovered) it terminated at Hilsea Garage – conveniently situated at the western end of Military Road – while on other occasions it turned round at Cosham Railway Bridge. When the bus came I put out my hand (as I had seen grown-ups do) and was somewhat amazed when it slowed down and stopped. It had not occurred to me that a ticket would be required, for I did not have any money, but a sympathetic conductor with an empty bus did not insist upon such formalities. Within five minutes I was deposited at Hilsea Garage, given a friendly pat on the head and told to run on home – which I did! Of course, the family were told all about this little adventure and henceforth I was allowed to have a few coppers whenever it was not possible for them to meet me, to legalise my unaccompanied bus travel.

Below: A selection of local tickets for buses, trams, ferries and trains. There is even one for the Woolston floating bridge./Author

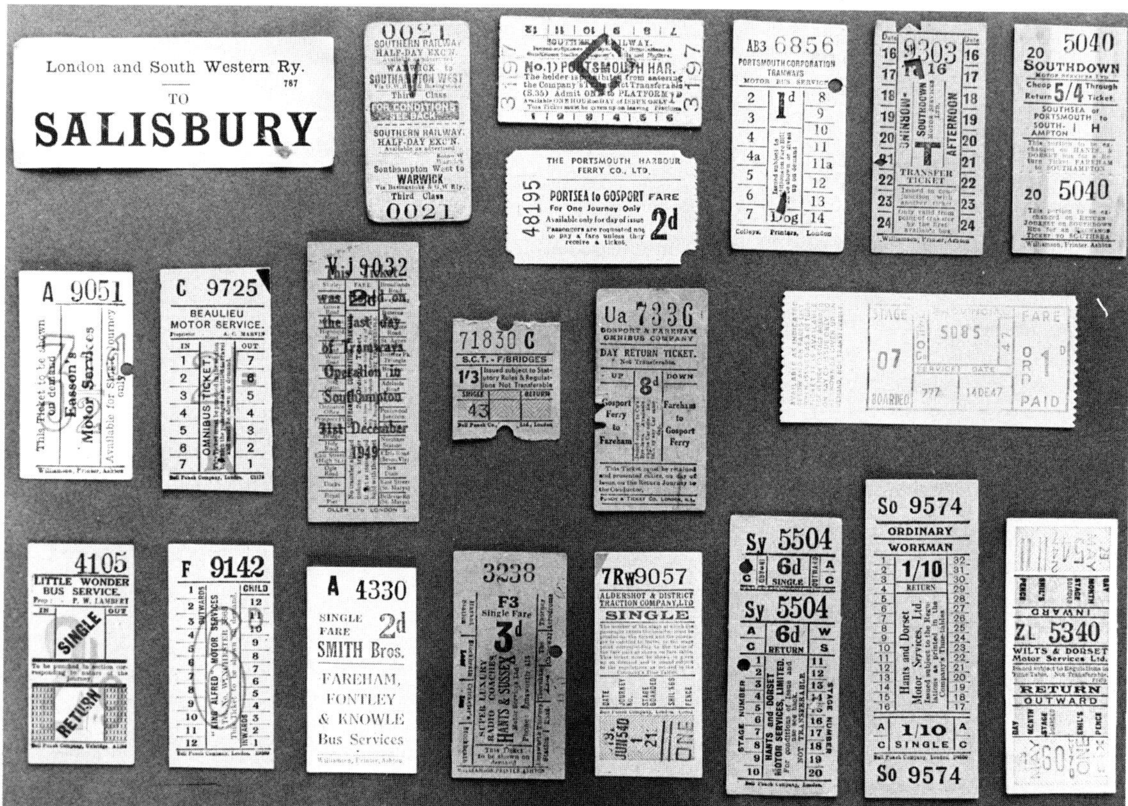

It was all rather exciting really. Suddenly a new kind of bus started to appear at Hilsea and, in my second year at school, I began to have lessons in the afternoons as well. Whilst this meant the curtailment of my pre-prandial jaunts – on which I soon contrived to obtain Bell-Punch Transfer tickets when the bus terminated at Cosham – there were to be other compensations. One day following afternoon school I walked up the lane towards Portsdown, with the intention of catching a bus down the hill instead of the familiar ride on the level from St Colman's. But drivers on Waterlooville, Horndean or Petersfield services must have been sceptical of a youngster with school satchel and cap trying to halt a bus in full flight on the descent; not one would stop for me. Fuming, I retraced my steps down Widley Lane to St Colman's and mumbled my displeasure to a Havant Road conductor! Tongue-in-cheek he suggested I should complain in the office at Hilsea; feeling indignant at being left high and dry at Widley, I marched into the office to be confronted by a rather pretty young lady whose name, I learned, was Maud Beryl May. Having told her in subdued tones of my experiences at the request stop, she suggested I might like to have a biscuit and share her cup of tea. Earlier disappointments were soon forgotten and an acquaintance was struck up that lasted till the family moved away to Fareham in 1948. Beryl (as she preferred to be called) rather spoiled me, I think; old timetables, handbills, ticket-rolls and other treasures found their way into my collection, while I soon became known to off-duty drivers and conductors as I looked wonderingly across the depot at all the fascinating buses garaged there. Soon I got to know their fleet-numbers and registrations, chassis types and body shapes, including the new 'utility' buses with their funny wooden seats and predominantly grey paintwork. If I was ever missing from home a quick telephone call to the garage nearly always succeeded in locating me, while Beryl was persuaded to impart to me the mysteries of Southdown's switchboard. They were very happy days in which I picked up my basic knowledge of buses in its green fleet, together with the knack of reading timetables or fare-charts and appreciating the finer points of destination screens. All these years later, I still retain a gratis copy of the last issue of a Southern Railway timetable dated October 1947 and a printed facsimile of a Portsmouth area destination-blind (PFF 41) as treasured souvenirs of many hours behind the counter at Hilsea Garage.

Readers may well have guessed the identity of some of the vehicles hinted at in these preceding anecdotes. In case there are any readers not quite certain what they were, let us take a closer look at a selection with knowledge of hindsight. Taking the double-deckers first, since they were my more usual kind of transport until changing schools in

Above left: St Colman's Church, bus-stop for Widley Lane. One of Southdown's last traditional buses, Leyland Titan PD3 No 263, features all-over advertising livery./*Author*

Left: Hilsea Garage, scene of many youthful delights. Southdown 'Convertible' open-top Leyland Titan PD3 No 412 has been prepared for Derby Day 1969, but is being used on relief duties in the interim./*Author*

SCREEN P.F.F.41.

PRIVATE

COSHAM
NORTH END
FRATTON BRIDGE
THEATRE ROYAL
VIA CASTLE STREET
PORTSMOUTH
THEATRE ROYAL
SOUTHSEA
VIA MAIN ROAD
COSHAM
PORTSMOUTH
(THEATRE ROYAL)
VIA CASTLE STREET
PORTSMOUTH
FRATTON BRIDGE
SOUTHSEA
VIA MAIN ROAD

45 PORTCHESTER FAREHAM
VIA CASTLE STREET

45A PORTCHESTER FAREHAM
WARSASH
VIA MAIN ROAD

45 PORTCHESTER
CORNAWAY LANE
VIA CASTLE STREET

45 PORTCHESTER
CROSS ROADS
VIA MAIN ROAD
PURBROOK
WATERLOOVILLE
VIA STAKES

39 WATERLOOVILLE DENMEAD HAMBLEDON
VIA MAIN ROAD

COWPLAIN
HORNDEAN
SNELLS CORNER
PETERSFIELD
VIA CLANFIELD
VIA HORNDEAN & SNELLS CORNER

LOVE DEAN
DRIFT ROAD
CLANFIELD

DRAYTON
FARLINGTON
HAVANT
EMSWORTH
CHICHESTER
WESTBOURNE

SOUTHWICK
WICKHAM
DROXFORD

1944, there were an assortment of middle-aged covered-top Leylands – all Titans – some of which were petrol TD1 or TD2 models, with the remainder being predominantly diesel-engined TD3, TD4 or TD5 varieties. A number of the petrol-engined 'cars', as Southdown call them to this day, were in the process of being re-bodied with utility Park Royal or East Lancs designs to replace their original Leyland or Short Brothers bodywork; the antique open-toppers retained their Brush bodies unaltered, save for the temporary canvas contraptions mentioned earlier. In subsequent years I managed to see all but one of Southdown's 23 examples, though there were many later covered-top versions that escaped me. A large number of TD1s in the 800 and 900 series had been withdrawn and sold prior to the outbreak of war and it is probable that the survivors were only reprieved on that account. Mechanically similar to but warmer than the Brush-bodied open-toppers thanks to their Clayton heaters, there was never the same thrill about a ride on these rebodied buses, particularly the ugly Park Royal examples – No 940 had been fitted with an East Lancs version that made it a much nicer looking

Above: Exact facsimile of the layout of a Southdown destination screen for the Portsmouth area, printed in 1941 (*PFF41*). It will be noted that route numbers were never used for incoming services until after the 1946 Co-Ordination Agreement with the Corporation. /*Author*

Right: A classic design of single-deck bus, Southdown's 1400-series have become a legend. Car 1464 of Petersfield undertakes a short working on service 60 as far as Trotton in 1951. /*Author*

Bottom right: An early essay into the mysteries of photography! Southdown's six Leyland Cub buses with half-cab Park Royal bodywork were always personal favourites. Only rarely did they stray from Hayling Island services – Nos 8 and 12 ventured as far as Portsmouth Dockyard on an excursion in the summer of 1951. /*Author*

bus altogether, while a handful of curious Willowbrook lowbridge rebuilds (mostly on TD2 chassis) were always interesting. I heard some of the drivers mutter darkly about certain oil-engined Titans with torque-converters – 'gearless' buses – but I never saw such vehicles in the Portsmouth area while still so equipped. Several oil-engined TD3 buses, dating from 1934, were regular performers on the service 45 to Fareham and Warsash; Nos 971, 973 and 975 spring to mind. Their highbridge Short Brothers bodywork had a sliding roof, but I don't recall it being opened at any time – it sounds a nice idea, though. Numbered from 100 upwards to 265 came a succession of TD4 and TD5 buses that were the 'standard' double-deckers of the immediate prewar years; some of the GCD-registered series were actually delivered after the outbreak of war in 1940. The variety of their bodywork was considerable and many were of lowbridge specification. Relatively few lowbridge buses were based in Portsmouth, since City routes were not restricted and most services radiating out could be worked by highbridge vehicles without difficulty. The 38 to Southwick, Wickham and Droxford (once operated by Blue Motors but absorbed in 1935) was often served by single-deckers but was also a preserve of local lowbridge operations. It was on this service, as a treat at holidays or autumn weekends, I would be taken to Southwick for rambles in the woods. Some of the lowbridge Titans had distinctive side destination-screens above the nearside windows: first the destination, then the route number and finally the intermediate points. Even in those days the 'via' blind might be left blank! The attraction for me of lowbridge buses was the sunken gangway upstairs, although this made it difficult for tall folk to get up from their seats on the lower deck without bumping their heads. On the upper deck all seats were to the left of the gangway in rows of three or four. Some lowbridge buses from Chichester or Bognor, working into Portsmouth on the famous 31 service, might also feature unusual advertisements. Perhaps utility Willowbrook buses like 949 or 951 might make a brief visit, although 953 spent some years based locally at Hilsea. Amongst all the different surviving body-styles – East Lancs, Beadle, Willowbrook, Shorts and Park Royal – the majority of more recent double-deckers (with FCD, FUF or GCD-registrations) were equipped with the last-named design as original equipment.

Single-deck buses were remarkably standardised, falling into two main categories only. There was a need for lightweight, petrol-engined buses for Hayling duties and these consisted of two kinds of Leyland Cub with both normal-control and forward-control chassis, all bodied by Park Royal. Only rarely did these appear in the City itself, practically their entire lives being spent based at Hayling or at Emsworth. The main brunt of single-deck operation was borne by a fleet of 86 superb Leyland Tiger TS7 and TS8 saloons with Harrington bodywork; early examples were petrol-engined with coach-seats for dual purpose-work, while the later series had less glazing round the rear and were equipped with oil engines. Even when fitted with perimeter seating as a means of carrying extra passengers during the war-time emergency, the 1400s were very superior vehicles. Like almost everything in the Southdown fleet, except the 1929 open-toppers already referred to, these Tigers were equipped with Clayton heaters on the front bulkhead at knee height. In common with the older double-deck buses, the 1400 series featured destination-screens above the nearside windows while all buses single- and double-deck alike (except the open-toppers) were provided with rear destination-screens. In the case of every single-decker it was located below the rear window, a view seldom shown in photographs.

During the period up to 1944 I had little contact with Southdown's coach fleet, which was much depleted by the requisitioning of petrol-engined vehicles by the War Department. This was a pleasure to be sampled once hostilities had ceased.

13
The Arab Invasion

Apart from D-Day, with its attendant build-up of military might both home produced and from the United States – much of which was temporarily stored along the roadsides throughout Hampshire, complete with crews – the summer of '44 was noted for the influx of a new breed of bus. Hinted at earlier, the delivery of 100 utility Guy Arab double-deckers to Southdown alone was indicative of the growing need for more mobility everywhere, now that the tide of war appeared to be on the turn after five long years. In addition, Hants & Dorset gained nine and Provincial 11 while Southampton Corporation obtained eight to add to their prewar collection of Guys. While referring to these somewhat unlikely machines, one should not omit mention of nine utility Daimlers purchased by Portsmouth Corporation (along with 10 petrol-engined OWB Bedford single-deckers). Likewise Provincial took delivery of a solitary Bristol K5G – not strictly a wartime chassis, but fitted with an 'unfrozen' Park Royal utility body – and Hants & Dorset clutched eagerly at a

Left: Though somewhat less gaunt than when delivered in 1944, there is no mistaking the utility ancestry of this pair of Southdown Guy Arabs found lurking at Hyde Park Road depot in 1957. Car 435 (GUF 135) represents the Northern Counties fashion while 481 (GUF 181, right) portrays the later Weymann style./*Author*

Right: Fareham bus station in 1946. Evidence of the recent war is found in the camouflaged Savoy cinema and two utility buses. The side entrance to the depot was used by Warsash-bound Southdown buses hourly, since they shared Hants & Dorset's bays opposite. The film at the Savoy was 'Dead of Night' with Michael Redgrave and Googie Withers.
/*The News, Portsmouth*

quartet of similar specification but with different bodywork. They also took seven 'genuine' all-utility Bristols, some of which were fitted with AEC 7.7 litre engines like Portsmouth's Daimlers. There had been a certain amount of inter-company borrowing, as when Portsmouth lent Southampton a trio of petrol-engined Tilling-Stevens double-deckers until their extra Guys appeared. Southdown had similarly borrowed from East Kent, but it is with the real wartime article that I shall be concerned here.

The only Mark I Arab to be used in the Portsmouth area was Provincial's 55 (EHO 228), delivered in 1942. Hants & Dorset received FRU 7-10 in the same year, followed by five DCR-registered buses in 1943; all gravitated to Eastleigh, where they were to spend the greater part of their lives with this operator. As with the great majority of double-deckers since the first covered-top examples, all were of lowbridge construction. Southdown was allocated only two Mark Is and these, together with the earliest Mark II models, went to the eastern part of its empire. But in 1944 six arrived at Hilsea! Numbered 410 to 413 (GUF 70-73), these Guys were normal

highbridge buses with utility Park Royal bodywork, whereas 414 and 415 (GUF 74/5) were fitted with lowbridge bodywork by Weymann – it was this pair that helped maintain the 38 service to Droxford for some years, but they remained unique in the Portsmouth area as the sole examples of austerity lowbridge buses. Thereafter deliveries came thick and fast, with several fitted with apparently narrow, angular bodies by Northern Counties. These were to prove a marvellous investment despite their ugly shape, for some remained at work in almost original condition for 20 years. Then came more Park Royal vehicles, popular with Southdown in later years for conversion to open-top, plus a goodly batch of less austere Weymann-bodied Guys that heralded the end of hostilities. . . .

There were some surprised looks when the Arabs started to appear. My recollection is of basically grey buses relieved by a couple of green bands, but photographic evidence of their early condition is not easy to come by. However, one of the Northern Counties buses turned up painted all-over grey with an unglazed upper-deck emergency 'window'! The Fareham road soon became their stronghold for, unless allocated to the once-hourly extension to Warsash, the route was totally flat with the exception of two railway 'hump' bridges. These were at Fratton and Wymering, for until the new dual carriageway through to Cosham was constructed in 1958 all A27 traffic used the narrow route past Sixth Avenue and the charming old Wymering Church. Starting at the foot of either bridge with a Gardner-engined vehicle – especially the 5-cylinder versions allocated to Portsmouth – meant staying in second gear until the summit. Anyone who has ever driven such a machine will know the problem of changing-up on hills, since road speeds drop quicker than engine speed preventing a noiseless movement through the gearbox. Beyond Fareham the route is shared with Hants & Dorset's service 77, to provide a half-hour frequency where Fuger had once tried to take on the giants! But whereas

Southdown was using new Guy Arabs — even if to utility specification – its neighbour was still relying on early Bristol Ks with Brush bodywork, or some antique petrol-engined Leylands. Both Bristols and Guys utilised the Gardner 5-cylinder diesel power unit of 7 litres capacity, which caused some grinding up Coach Hill or Titchfield Hill in either case. But gradients or not, there was one driver working for Southdown who became something of a folk-hero to school-boys in the late 1940s and 1950s, when it came to driving Guys. He alone, it seemed, had the wit to make them really go – he was a big man, with a small beard as I recall, with the strength to make the Arabs lean over precariously when cornering fast. I have sat behind him, in the front passenger seat on the lower deck, watching the speed-ometer flick into action as he began to wind his bus up through the gears; along the waterfront at Paulsgrove the needle would hover around the '40' mark, regardless of a standing load, with the transmission whis-tling and whining as only Guys can. There was nothing he liked better than three bells ('full up') from his conductor — one was seldom late with him!

Portsmouth Corporaton Daimlers were very much a minority group when it came to comparisons of austerity buses in the Solent area. There were only nine, with utility double-deck bodies by Duple. They, too, were painted grey but with red bands and spent most of their earlier years on Copnor Road routes A and B, or between Highbury Estate and Wymering on services J and K. As no Corporation bus was equipped with a saloon heater until the third series of post-war PD2s in 1958, in winter it was much nicer to travel on a cosy Southdown vehicle – nearly all of which had lower-deck heaters from 1930 onwards. My impressions of Corporation buses in those days were influenced by such considerations – rather unfairly, I tended to think of them as 'second class' machines by Southdown stan-dards. But if that was so, I must add that Provincial buses in my youthful eyes were certainly 'third class' – in no way a reflection

on their reliability, but just schoolboy pre-judice and favouritism. To return for a moment to the Portsmouth Daimlers, they were CWA6 models with traditional fluid flywheel and Wilson pre-select gearbox. Their acceleration was bettered only by a few petrol-engined buses, though one had to hang on for dear life until top gear was achieved for the 'snatch' could be as lively as a trolley bus. They retained their wooden slatted seats longer than Southdown's Guys – after rebodying by Crossley in 1955 their appearance was transformed and, like many other Corporation buses, they topped a score of years in traffic.

Finally, I must not leave out the little Bedford OWB single-deckers purchased by the Corporation between November 1942 and April 1944. Two were bodied by Mulliner and the rest by Duple with the usual austerity expected at the time, being numbered 161 to 170 with various registrations in the CTP-series. No 161 (CTP 3) was delivered in grey livery, the remainder in brown; these disguises were worn for the duration of the war, whereupon they were found useful on a variety of peace-time duties such as 'short' workings between Guildhall and Old Portsmouth, Wymering and Upper Drayton or Milton and Tipner. Though I never had cause to travel upon an OWB, the distinctive sound in indirect gears was part of their charm and we are the poorer for their going in 1963. Other Bedfords of the same type were used by various branches of the armed forces at a number of establishments around the Solent; one, for-merly allocated to the Royal Air Force, ended its days as a school bus operated on behalf of West Sussex County Council in the late 1960s, based at a garage at Trotton. Finally put out to grass beneath the ample cover of a centenarian oak, it lingered in a state of suspended animation for several years – complete with original slatted seats and petrol engine – until happily rescued for long term restoraton and preservation by a member of the Vintage Transport Associ-ation in 1975.

14
Homeward Bound from Grove Road South

With the war drawing to a close, I started attending St John's College in Southsea as a junior from the autumn term of 1944. This meant all sorts of exciting changes, apart from the wearing of an official school uniform of blazer, cap and tie! To begin with I needed a season ticket each term, for the journey was four miles each way from Hilsea; in theory there was a choice between the Corporation services and Southdown – they did not become Joint until 1946 – but with Beryl to advise me that aspect of the matter was academic. . . . Most of the teachers at St John's were Brothers of the De La Salle Order, a most dedicated, humane and Christian group of people who could unravel the mysteries of mathematics and French, English or Latin whilst maintaining a balance between humour and discipline with total *aplomb*. Sure as the sunrise, every day began with a bus ride and every lesson with a 'Hail, Mary'. There was homework to be done most evenings, but time enough for a look round the depot each night and listen to Dick Barton on the radio at 6.45pm. The mornings were always a scramble, dashing off down Military Road to the bus-stop to join a queue with office workers, shop assistants and several other school-children for a 20 minute ride to Southsea.

Seldom was there much time to spare on these occasions and, at first, I concentrated on just getting to school as quickly as poss-ible. Situated as it was in Grove Road South – between Elm Grove and Palmerston Road – there were a number of permutations for the journey, but the element of choice was more often than not dictated by considerations of space! Nothing to do with satellites or heavenly bodies, the question of space related simply to the degree of over-crowding that each conductor would permit on his bus. The official dictum at that time was eight standing passengers but few conductors interpreted it literally. Ten adults was the 'norm' but children only paid half so they only counted as half, or so it seemed. The queue became shorter as each bus filled to the brim; the passing of minutes felt like hours while the big hand of the clock on Southdown's building edged nearer towards nine o'clock. The matter of not being late was influenced in a devious way by the weekly 'testimonial', since lateness, inferior work or misbehaviour might result in a white or (horror of horrors!) green instead of the acceptable blue or (excellent) red testimonial to one's parents. Whether local bus conductors were a party to this cunning device I rather doubt, but be it said, they rarely turned away anxious schoolchildren if they could avoid it. On more than one occasion, to avoid detection by an inspector, two or three of us were shepherded into the darkness under the staircase. This was quite fun in fine weather, but if it was raining and one was travelling on an '800' (whose staircase was open to the elements) the effect could be ruinous and require an instant visit to the washroom on arrival!

The most direct means of reaching Grove Road South was a Southdown bus via Fratton Road and Elm Grove – provided by services 31A/B, 41, 43 and 45 (the last mentioned was not re-routed via Victoria Road South to The Circle until 1958). Corporation motor bus A reached the same destination via Commercial Road and King's Road, but there were problems with services using this route before nine o'clock each morning, as they were diverted at the Royal Hospital to travel along Flathouse Road and Unicorn Gate to Edinburgh Road before resuming their proper course. It might have been useful for Dockyard personnel but it was a dreaded delay to pupils with roll-call awaiting them. Other alternatives were by trolley bus to Victoria Road South (Elm Grove corner) with a brisk walk through The Thicket and in by the back way, or a Southdown bus via Commercial Road (and the Unicorn Gate deviation) on services 31, 40 or 42. These three services travelled past the Town station (Portsmouth & Southsea station, to give it its full title), Guildhall, Theatre Royal, the Terraces and Kent Road; one got off at St Jude's Church on the corner of Palmerston Road, with the prospect of a headlong gallop past Marmion Road to the school. I was hardly ever late until my final term in 1948, by which time the family had moved to Fareham involving a much longer journey.

But it was the journey home at the conclusion of afternoon school that gave the greatest pleasure. Gone was the sense of urgency; time was no longer of the essence and, so long as I was home for tea, I might take what route I pleased. Southdown provided a bus at 3.45pm outside the gates as a scholars' special, bound for Havant as an extra 31B. As we scampered out of the gates, almost anything might be waiting for us across the road: frequently it was a 'standee' 1400-series Leyland Tiger TS7 or TS8 single-decker, but any one of the

Above: Morning rush-hour in Commercial Road, Portsmouth, about 1945. I can count 12 buses – including the RN Bedford OWB in the foreground – in an assortment of styles and liveries.
/*The News, Portsmouth*

double-deckers might be turned out instead – it was anyone's guess. About the same time as the school bus was scheduled to depart, a service 43 double-decker would arrive from South Parade Pier for Westbourne, thus providing an excuse for a certain amount of leap-frogging at bus-stops until either (or both) became full. One could be certain that, if they were still not full up by the time they reached Kingston Cross, they surely would be on leaving North End Junction! One summer afternoon I was on the upper deck of No 208

(FCD 508) travelling northwards along Fratton Road when it pulled up at a request stop. Almost at once there was a crash followed by the sound of broken glass – of course, all the passengers looked to see what had happened. The shapely radiator of a Corporation Leyland Cheetah (No 44) was close enough to touch through the back window, while fragments of glass were scattered all over the staircase and platform! There was a short pause while all and sundry inspected the damage, making *sotto voce* remarks about the comparative merits of the two vehicles concerned to the detriment of the Cheetah, before clambering back on board to resume the journey. At Hilsea another bus was waiting to replace the battle-scarred 208. After all the other passengers had changed over, I remained on board as it went round the long narrow roundabout (where once the trams had run) and into the depot for examination and repair. Needless to say Beryl wanted to know all about it, while car 208 became mildly famous for its encounter. It was quite sad when its original Park Royal body was replaced some years later by one of East Lancs manufacture.

After the Coordination Agreement was authorised between Portsmouth Corporation and Southdown in 1946 it was possible to sample a much wider choice of vehicles. In addition, I became a member of St John's College choir, with the result that on one or two evenings a week I might be required for practice and so be unable to catch the usual bus home. On these occasions I would walk to the Theatre Royal for the 'Rush-hour Show'. I have hinted before that rush-hour reliefs were a feature of the times and, with no private motoring, bus and train services had a virtual monopoly of the traffic. Yet although one might have to wait up to an hour to get on to a bus, no one ever failed to get home if they were patient. Southdown had six bus-stops outside the Theatre Royal for all their various destinations, but as I was free to catch any one for Hilsea, I used to dash from one to the other just as my fancy took me. The attraction, of course, was the most interesting vehicle available and during the evening peak Hyde Park

Below: Evening rush-hour. Every night there were queues outside the Theatre Royal, Portsmouth. The Short Bros bodywork of car 974 and Bisto advertisement are typical of the 1940s period, but the destination indicator has not been changed since the morning peak!/*The News, Portsmouth*

Above: One of those petrol-engined tourers . . . Car 1130 (CCD 730) was a typical Harrington-bodied example with folding canvas roof, used on rush-hour limited stop journeys to Cowplain and beyond. /*Southdown Motor Services Ltd*

Road might push out practically anything! Unlike the school buses, they were not limited to traditional double-deckers or single-deck 1400s: it was from Hyde Park Road that one might travel home in style on board one of the lovely prewar coaches. . . . However, there was a snag – as I discovered the first time I succeeded in getting on one! The coach in question was one of the petrol-engined tourers with folding canvas roof, a Harrington creation on a Leyland Tiger TS7 or TS8 chassis and numbered somewhere in the 1100-series – it was growing dark and with all the people milling about I never noticed which one it was. I contrived to get somewhere near the front within reach of the Clayton heater, for it was filling up fast and in no time at all three bells rang out to indicate it was full up. With that magical hiss, the petrol engine roared into life with a puff of blue smoke and we were off. Up through the gears it went in its exhilarating way, without more ado, and I thought it was great fun not having to stop tediously here and there as no one seemed to want to get off. When it went sailing

through North End Junction without stopping I was amazed, for nothing – but nothing – failed to pull in there! That should have warned me all was not what it seemed, but when I began to edge my way towards the rear to get off at Hilsea I came face to face with the conductor, who told me in no uncertain terms that Cowplain was the first stop. Anxiously I waited near the door but the Tiger passed everything in sight, storming Portsdown as though it had developed wings. Passing Purbrook and Waterlooville in fine style, my heart was in my mouth as I wondered when I would ever get home, especially without much money, but at last the pace slackened and the conductor grinned as he opened the door for me. 'You had better catch the school bus next time, my lad' he quipped, before adding more kindly, 'You'll find a bus going back to Hilsea in a few minutes across the road'. The coach disappeared into the darkness like a dream, with nothing but lingering petrol fumes to confirm that I had not just been spirited out to Cowplain by magic. Crossing the road carefully, I found the bus-stop and waited. In scarcely more than five minutes a friendly, familiar shape loomed up out of the gloom, a tall-masted creation with flapping canvas like the vessel in Wagner's 'Flying Dutchman' – dear old 801, thank God! I crept upstairs, hoping that no one would want to look at my pass, but I

84

was in luck that night and 801 had the wind under its tail, so I was back at Hilsea hardly half an hour later than expected. The tale had to be told at home and again next day for Beryl's benefit, but at least it taught me what to expect in the rush-hour – a foretaste of today's limited stop services.

Subsequently, becoming fascinated by the goings-on at Hyde Park Road, I used to go there quite regularly. At the peak, buses and coaches would come pouring out of the depot in a seemingly endless queue, all belching exhaust fumes where they had just been started 'cold' after hours of idleness – black smoke from the diesels and blue from the petrol vehicles. Practically anything that would go might be turned out: ancient Tiger coaches (TS2s of 1930) with Coventry-style radiators such as 1004 or 1005, a good cross section of prewar double-deckers or even the classic band-box Harrington coach 1211 (EUF 511). This was possibly my all time favourite coach, built with an oil engine from new and always maintained in immaculate condition – what a shame it was never preserved! On the other hand, one summer evening even a Cub took me home, the only occasion I can ever recall travelling on one of the six forward-control Park Royal buses away from Hayling Island (car No 8; DUF 8). But I am neglecting to mention some of the more interesting vehicles in the Corporation fleet, upon which I was now permitted to travel to or from school, thanks to the Co-ordination Agreement. Leaving aside the trolley buses until a later chapter, as well as the utility vehicles already referred to, the active Corporation fleet in the 1944-1948 period was full of interest, if lacking quite the almost mystical appeal of Southdown. With the benefit of my recent research into material kept by the City Record Office I am bound to say that photographs of Corporation buses prior to World War II show them to have been kept in truly splendid condition. It took a number of years of peace to restore these vehicles to the same standard after the battering suffered in the interim, a factor I did not appreciate as a child. But, in their grey-painted, rundown state they still provided a service with few known failures, reflecting much credit on Ben Hall and his staff at Eastney and North End.

Looking back, I realise how lucky I was to see so many old stagers running in virtually original condition. Although I am unable to remember the 1930s, before my eyes was a complete cross-section of that decade's development. There were petrol-engined Leyland Titan TD1s, with the choice of Park Royal, Short Brothers or English Electric bodywork, favoured for use on cross-town routes such as E and F, G or H. One was particularly notable for the following reason. As with many operators, the Corporation had tried to economise on petrol during the war by employing some gas-producers attached as trailers to several of the older buses. In order to overcome loss of power, engines were bored out and oversize pistons used; naturally, when conditions improved, these buses returned to normal petrol fuel with engines sleeved to standard bore once again. At least, all but one were reconverted. The exception was, I believe, No 91 recognisable to the keen observer by its speedometer – stuck fast at over 60mph, a reminder of a quick run along the Eastern Road one day after its bored-out engine had been blessed again with proper fuel! At any rate, that was the tale handed down to an inquisitive schoolboy and who will gain-say it now? There were a dozen similar buses (Nos 16-27) that were fuelled by diesel, being very early examples of Leyland's option offered on a TD2 chassis. With customary good husbandry at Eastney depot, a couple of these 1933 vehicles remained in service till 1958, while two more became part of the service stock as tower wagons to survive into today's 'preservation age'. But the truly marvellous oil-engined buses were Portsmouth's first Crossleys. After the experimental purchase of one AEC Regent and one Crossley Condor in 1931 for comparative evaluation, it was decided to obtain 20 more Condors in 1932 (fleet Nos

95-114). The production batch featured familiar English Electric bodywork of the period, hardly distinguishable from the TD1s or TD2s, whereas both 1931 experimental buses were bodied by Shorts. The solitary Regent was lost in the bombing, while the prototype Condor No 74 (RV 720) outlived all eventualities – although with shortened chassis and cut down for use as a lorry – to be the only survivor of its breed, now in the care of Portsmouth Museums. I did not manage to obtain many rides on them, for they appeared only during the rush-hour or as football specials to Fratton Park on Saturdays, but once seen they were never likely to be forgotten! The gearlever was on the driver's right – like a Black Label Bentley – with gate-change box. The transmission produced a unique sound that I would liken to a grinding noise, always accompanied by generous exhaust emission that would do credit to a coal-fired steam engine. As on a number of early buses, Leyland TD1s included, the accelerator pedal was in between clutch and brake, something that could not have contributed to easy driving especially when allied to the position of the gearlever referred to above. How quaint they must have seemed to Corporation drivers after no less than 46 Titan TD4s entered the fleet from 1935 onwards! The TD4 was so robust, so predictable, that it survived in revenue-earning service until 1972. Three sorts of bodywork were fitted and it is interesting to note that the earliest by English Electric (on Nos 115-126) is the only variety to have survived into preservation. Four all metal Leyland-bodied buses (Nos 127-130) gave over 20 years service each, with 130 retaining original appearance until withdrawal in 1960. The largest batch comprised the 30 Craven-bodied buses purchased to finally oust the trams in 1936, numbered 131-160. They gave sterling service to the City until modern Leyland Titan PD2 buses came into use but, even then, their influence lingered on – salvaged transmission and engine units were used to re-equip a postwar series of all-Crossley buses fitted with Turbomotors, when these proved unequal to the task. Like their trolley counterparts, the Cravens were the 'standard' Corporation bus until new deliveries began in 1948, one lasting in service until 1960 in original condition (No 146; RV 9400). My favourite was No 160, a bus that always seemed clean and well cared for even in early postwar days. On my first ever visit to Eastney depot I was allowed to sit in its cab and start the engine – quite a thrill at 10 years old! More than a quarter of a century was to pass before an opportunity presented itself to drive a prewar Leyland Titan again. . . .

Left: Portsdown Hill in the 1940s. As new pre-fabs are built on the lower slopes near Widley Lane, a Southdown Leyland TD5 with Park Royal double-deck body surmounts the gruelling climb to 'The George'. /*The News, Portsmouth*

15
A Matter of Class

At almost the same time as Portsmouth began to receive deliveries of its first postwar double-deckers, 25 Leyland Titan PD1 or PD1A oil-engined vehicles with either Metro-Cammell Weymann or locally built Readings bodywork (numbered 180-200 and 1-4), my family moved house in April 1948. I could never remember moving before and it was a challenging experience. While, on the one hand, there were all the new places to explore, yet there was sadness at saying goodbye to old friends and familiar haunts. If the distance involved was only eight miles out to Catisfield (near Fareham), it was still the harbinger of even greater changes to come.

For the summer term of 1948 I had to make the daily journey to St John's from Catisfield by bus. Perhaps the earlier start required convinced me, once and for all, that I am a 'night' person; in any case it was necessary to catch a bus into Fareham at a sufficiently early hour to make connection with the 'official' school bus, which left at 8 o'clock from the bus station. Luckily, Southdown relied heavily on the petrol-engined Titan TD1s for such tasks despite their being 18 or 19 years old. The 45A service ran via Castle Street to Portchester and then via Fratton Road to Portsmouth, while the through Warsash bus (service 45) took the main road route at Portchester followed by Commercial Road and Guildhall to South Parade Pier in the City. White

Hart Lane was not a made-up road at that stage, having a sort of shingle surface between Castle Street and Cornaway Lane. It was decided to resurface it during that summer term, with consequent diversions while work was in progress. Buses ran as far as they could from Cornaway Lane along White Hart Lane before turning round, then retraced the ground to the main road, which was followed into Portchester. However, at the Crossroads, the bus would turn south into Castle Street and call at all usual stops to the turning for White Hart Lane before continuing along the lower part of Castle Street – not normally served by buses – to turn round again practically in the shadow of the ancient castle's walls. One wonders what Roman centurions would have thought of this landward 'invasion'! Unfortunately I have not been able to find any photographs of this unusual temporary arrangement, although some Corporation 'ultimate' destination-blinds included Portchester Castle amongst their selection.

On arrival at Fareham from Portsmouth on anything but the hourly through service 45 to Warsash, one was presented with a change of bus and of operator. The old bus station on the corner of Portland Street was very cramped as it dated from 1930, causing Southdown buses terminating there to reverse before being able to extricate themselves – they used to enter the bus station from the front, opposite the Savoy cinema.

The exception was the Warsash bus, which turned down Portland Street and entered from a side entrance immediately in front of the depot, which housed Hants & Dorset's motley collection, before pulling up on 'their' side adjoining the Wesleyan Church. I had made a few journeys to Locks Heath whilst living at Hilsea, mostly travelling by Southdown bus right through, but the one or two trips that had involved changing at Fareham had been full of interest. The remainder of this chapter will be devoted to a nostalgic review of Hants & Dorset as I found it on moving to Catisfield in the spring of 1948.

Rather like Portsmouth Corporation, 'H&D' had some villainous old buses – both single- and double-deck – still theoretically operational, as well as its first influx of modern, standardised vehicles of Bristol manufacture. Most readers will be aware of the significance of the two controlling groups in the bus industry outside London and the municipalities: British Electric Traction and Tilling. Within the geographical boundaries of this book Southdown and Aldershot & District belonged to BET while Hants & Dorset was part of the latter organisation. Whereas Southdown was meticulous about the display of destinations, its neighbour would paint them over as soon as look at them – sometimes. Until the end of 1949 the fleet numbering system used by Hants & Dorset was a tangled web of individual classes, using fine shaded transfers and lending an air of distinction to some otherwise shabby old buses. The Fareham allocation was not large, since it needed to cater for a modest area with routes to Warsash, Lee-on-the-Solent, Hill Head, Burridge and Bishop's Waltham. Single-deckers consisted of a handful of prewar Bristol L5G saloons with front-entrance Beadle bodywork with a couple of postwar examples bodied by Eastern Coachworks to help them out, while the double-deck fleet comprised two 1930 period pieces (in the shape of Leyland Titan TD1 petrol buses) supported by two Brush-bodied Bristol K5Gs of 1938 and some later Eastern Coachworks examples on the same prewar chassis. To the foregoing list must be added two new Bristol Ks and an odd trio of Leyland Lion saloons, whose sole purpose in life appeared to be catering for the squatters at Green Woods or as reliefs to HMS *Collingwood*. It was to this assorted collection that I was introduced on taking up residence at Catisfield!

With my predilection for petrol buses, I was delighted to find that the two antique Titans normally handled the 75 service from Fareham to Hill Head via Titchfield. E 306 (TK 3884) was preferred, since its Leyland bodywork retained many classic features including 'piano-front' and simple destination screens at front and rear. As almost all Hants & Dorset double-deckers were low-bridge, with the exception of two small classes I shall come to later when referring to Southampton, I became familiar with sunken gangways and seats for four upstairs. E 332 had been partly rebuilt by ECW after the war and had a modified destination layout at the front with nothing at all behind – foretaste of the 1970s. In service there was little to choose between them, but E 332 could always be heard back-firing when descending the hill into Titchfield. Route numbers were seldom displayed on prewar buses: none of the single-deckers had facilities for it while the Bristol Ks did have a small aperture (both front and rear) but this generally showed blank, perhaps because of subsequent route renumbering. The two Brush-bodied Ks, numbered TD 632/634 (BTR 309/310) were a bit ponderous after riding on Southdown Guys and both had notices in the driver's cab with the injunction 'Not to be used on Lymington service'. I have never been able to find out why this was so, or whether similar strictures applied to any other vehicles – I cannot imagine the Gardner 5LW engine being unable to cope with Lymington's hill, steep though it is! It was not often I had an opportunity to ride on a single-decker, as they mostly worked the 73 service to Lee-on-the-Solent via Peel Common and Stubbington or its associated route (73A) to Hill Head. Once I managed a ride to Green Woods on the petrol-engined Leyland Lion LT5A type, being the sole passenger on the return journey aboard BA 78. In my youthful ignorance, I assumed the vehicle to be a Cheetah like Southdown's Hayling Island coaches or Portsmouth Corporation's first postwar Sea Front buses. Seldom was I able to procure a ride on the prewar Bristol Ls, but one lunchtime trip to Lee-on-the-Solent made the journey via Titchfield so I hitched a ride with TS809 (FLJ 436) from the bus station. Standing near the entrance and peering over the driver's shoulder, I could just see the speedometer (which was practically obscured by the low windscreen). As the bus charged under the railway arch in top gear, I was amazed to hear him change UP – it was one of a handful fitted with an overdrive 5th, it transpired.

One benefit of travelling by Hants & Dorset bus from Fareham, if you collected bus tickets, was the chance of obtaining a selection of old-style Bell Punch examples in assorted colours. Apart from the green 1d issued for half-fares from Fareham to the top of Titchfield Hill (Catisfield side), one's collection might be further augmented by surreptitious raiding of every used-ticket box that came to hand! I have recently surprised several friends in the Vintage Transport Association – who are ardent ticket enthusiasts of many years' standing – with some hitherto-undiscovered varieties filched in this manner 30 years ago. . . . Special protective fares used to be charged on some routes, while over-printed tickets for use on certain joint sections – for example, within the Borough of Gosport – were also issued. It was a sad day when those colourful and distinctive Bell Punch tickets ceased, although there was an overlap period during which they remained valid alongside the Insert Setright variety – themselves quite presentable and long since replaced by flimsy paper things!

Although Fareham's 'stud' of buses was relatively modest and unremarkable, there were some interesting visitors on routes operated by other Hants & Dorset depots. The Winchester service (69) was sometimes extended to Gosport, with a protective fare, running directly down the main road from Fareham until reaching Gosport's railway station, where it turned along Spring Garden Lane and then into Walpole Road. In later years this extension to Gosport was transferred to the 76 service, itself by then enlarged into a fully-fledged route between Fareham and Southampton via Burridge and Botley. But in the late 1940s the Winchester service might provide an assortment of Bristol K5G vehicles from the 1938 series, some registered BTR and others JT, all with Brush bodywork. On the other hand, instead of a TD class Bristol, there might be a Leyland Titan TD2 with Brush lowbridge styling but having only a single destination aperture (no via blind or route number) to distinguish it. Most of these 'M' class Leylands had been equipped with Gardner 5LW diesel engines prior to the war and their guttural growl was slightly different from the K5G. On the upper deck each row of seats alternated in providing for three or four passengers, the total being 52 on both decks. Most of the Ms were re-bodied in 1949 by Eastern Coachworks and the distinctive conical interior lights fitted by their original bodybuilder were lost in the process. No doubt their regular passengers appreciated a brighter-lit interior at night, but what character had been created by Brush!

Without doubt, the route for variety and interest par excellence was the 80 between Fareham and Woolston. Until the closure of the latter's depot in the Seventies, practically all duties on this service were operated from there; Woolston also seemed to attract the oldest vehicles, which made it an ideal venue for an outing. In the next chapter let us take a nostalgic ride from Fareham to Woolston and on to Southampton, in the days before the new Itchen Bridge and supremacy of the motor car.

16
By Bus, Floating Bridge and Tram to Southampton

The year is 1948; Woolston buses leave Fareham at eight minutes past practically every hour of the working day. For me, during the school holidays, it's a good idea to make a day of it. Waiting at the bus-stop at the top of Catisfield Hill – that's the Fareham side of Titchfield, on the A27 main road – one would see Southdown's 45 service come along every hour on the hour, usually a bright green and cream Guy with correct destination displays for Warsash at front, side and rear. Ten minutes after, for the 80 was never late, the unmistakable outline of a Beadle lowbridge double-decker in a more sombre shade of green would appear in the distance along the half mile of straight road. Holding one's sandwiches carefully with the right hand in order to signal the driver with the left, there is some screeching of brakes as an elderly Leyland Titan TD2 pulls up. Commonly G136 or G350 (LJ 5018/9), one dives quickly inside to bag the seat behind the driver, beneath the sunken upper deck gangway. Starting away in second gear, the growl of a Gardner diesel sounds strange coming from a Leyland's transmission, but in a moment the bus is coasting down the old narrow road into Titchfield across the river Meon. Taking the blind right-angle bend past the Abbey Restaurant with due caution, third gear's roar echoes back from narrow streets as, with more squealing from the brakes, our 'G' comes to rest in The Square. But

what's all this? With conductor holding up the traffic, the bus is turned round to face the way we have just come! On restarting, third gear is held for a sharp left turn and equally sharp ascent of Southampton Hill before the main A27 is rejoined. Passing Titchfield's RAF camp to the north, the bus swings away from the main road again into Lower Church Road and stops at Dimmick's Corner. Turning right into Hunt's Pond Road, the route becomes common once more with the Warsash service as far as Park Gate. Keeping straight ahead now along the A27 – passing Cold East Hospital and Sarisbury Green – the bus descends the long, winding hill to Bursledon where, not so many years before, there had been a timber bridge astride the Hamble river. Up and down the switch-back of slopes, the 80 finally leaves the main road at Lowford; there is a deceptive climb to the staggered crossroads for Hamble, but the aged vehicle keeps straight ahead with few stops until Sholing is reached. Dropping sharply under the chestnut trees, there is a sudden crackle from the exhaust as power is applied again for the final rise before Woolston. Stops are more frequent now until, spread out below like a model, the Itchen waterfront extends full width from left to right. The bus turns right to descend the hill beside the railway station – an area well blasted by German bombers only six or seven years before – to terminate across the road from Hants &

Dorset's compound in preparaton for the next journey back to Fareham. My souvenir of the trip is a white 8d single ticket, as there are no child return fares, but there is a wonderful assortment of used tickets of all colours in the box. . . .

Across the road there are a couple more 'G' Leylands for Hamble services (81 and 81A), while the depot houses an 'M' and maybe a couple of Leyland-bodied 'E' double-deckers plus a sagging 'BG' single-deck Lion. The last-mentioned vehicle once ventured as far as Fareham on a rush-hour relief – a fantastic sight with its revolving roof-mounted ventilators! But one must hurry down the ramp to catch the floating bridge across the river to Southampton. Up goes the black ball at the front and, with one gate already shut, the bridge makes steam and sets out for the opposite shore. Foot passengers can travel free: as the metal hawser begins to slide under the guide-wheel, water gurgles and surges under the bridge and the voyage has begun. In mid-channel the two bridges will pass and then power is shut off and no sound heard, save for the rumble of the hawser in its guides and water lapping all around. With a rasp the bridge grounds on the western shore, gates open and people pour off making for the buses nearby. Southampton Corporation services 1 and 3 will take passengers into the centre of the town, travelling there-after by a circuitous route over Northam Bridge and round to Woolston on the eastern shore. In their brighter livery of crimson and cream with aluminium roofs, these buses make a complete contrast with Hants & Dorset's green, but prewar Leylands are evident here too. With their attractive Park Royal bodies (highbridge, naturally), the Leyland TD4 and TD5 models have much in common with their opposite numbers in Portsmouth or with Southdown, but all are oil-engined and seem rather basic inside with their plain leather seats, with huge knobs instead of handles or rails to hold on to. Finding my favourite seat behind the driver, one is struck with the blue-tinted window to avoid glare at night from interior lights. Almost at once, driver and conductor appear and there is a roar as the hefty engine bursts into life. At seemingly breakneck speed, the Titan leaps away and hustles along over uneven surfaces rather worse than in Portsmouth. The pace of life seems alto-gether faster in Southampton as one catches a first glimpse of trams – gaunt and grey, like some storm-tossed battleship that has found safe harbour. Up through the bomb-scarred streets the bus rattles and sways till one is deposited in New Road, adjoining Above Bar. Here there is time to catch

Left: A Southampton Corporation Leyland TD5, No 25 (CTR 505) in postwar red and cream livery on service 3. /*N. Hamshere*

one's breath and admire the attractive setting with trees and greenery all around.

Soon enough the eye will be caught by the endless succession of red and green buses crossing and recrossing this busy junction close by the Civic Centre – where are they all coming from? In the case of the green Hants & Dorset buses, at least, the answer is not hard to find; just round the corner towards the railway station is the Bus Station at West Marlands, a veritable hive of activity and variety. Apart from the bus stands within, it appears that buses have their departure points from any spare piece of pavement nearby. More H&D classes will be found, like the postwar Leyland PD1s on the service 47 to Winchester – appropriately known as the PD type – while services to Romsey or into the New Forest may produce prewar Leylands of all sorts from TD1 to TD4. In addition to the E, G and M classes met already, at Southampton and (more rarely) at Woolston one might find the pre-Tilling 'standard' of class 'A'. By this period a choice of three engines might be in use in this collection of Titan TD3 and TD4 models, although most would have been delivered with Leyland

Above: A peaked-cap Leyland, typical of many Hants & Dorset TD1 buses of class 'E'. No E354 (LJ 2941) and Brush-bodied TD2 (M158; LJ 7096) wait for customers to Eastleigh at West Marlands bus station, Southampton in 1948./*A. B. Cross*

Above right: Although photographed at West Marlands as late as 1959, both Bristol K5G double-deckers 1053 and 1091 are recognisable as of prewar manufacture. Until 1950 they were numbered in the TD class by Hants & Dorset./*Author*

petrol units and some with torque-converters (especially for the Poole tramways replacement), but latterly Gardner 5LW, Leyland 8.6 litre or E181 (postwar) 7.4 litre diesels were used. One or two even had their petrol engines refitted just prior to disposal and I came across one still carrying class 'P' transfers (intended to distinguish torque-converter models). But, as rush-hour loomed, a towering AEC Regent with Tilling highbridge bodywork and open curving staircase might appear; Hants & Dorset borrowed three from Brighton, Hove & District after the war and decided to buy them two years later, whereupon they became S517, S519 and

S521. To complete the line-up of older buses would be two types of single-deck Leyland, comprising a pair of Cubs with normal-control chassis and Beadle coachwork (L998/9; CCR 856/7) that might appear on journeys between Southampton Central station and the Royal Pier (service 52) plus several 'BB' class Lions rebodied by Beadle with bus bodies incorporating full rear destination indicators! More modern vehicles in evidence would be an increasing volume of standard Bristol Ks with pleasing Eastern Coachworks lowbridge double-deck bodywork, all allotted TD class numbers, in addition to the 1938-1940 series mentioned earlier. These buses were providing regular services to Lymington and Bournemouth (services 19/20) as well as helping the PD class on Winchester duties (services 47/48). They were also appearing increasingly on the 70 service to Gosport and the 53/54 to Fareham. On the 53, particularly, one might see TD783; this had been fitted with an experimental 6-cylinder Bristol AVW engine and its progress was carefully monitored for two years before further orders were placed for production models of the

K6B. Before finally dragging myself away, an even wider assortment of Bell Punch tickets could be found including return fares of as much as five shillings, presumably on the complete Bournemouth-Southampton journey.

Walking through the back streets to Above Bar, only a brief wait would be necessary before catching a tram to Bassett and Swaythling. Nearly all those I saw were of domed-roof design, introduced by Mr P. Baker in 1923 for passing through the Bargate. Clambering aboard, every tram seemed full of people. With characteristic sounds it would commence its rolling gait, making its way northward into London Road before tackling the long but gentle ascent through The Avenue. Though I have been privileged to make only a few tram journeys in Britain (other than on preserved cars at Crich), the ride along The Avenue on a Southampton Corporation tramcar must have a very special place in my memories. At Bassett crossroads it would squeal on the sharp curve eastward into Burgess Road, which it followed to journey's end at Swaythling. As I recall, Southampton tram fares nearly always ended in an odd ½d while their tickets – though not as prolific in their variety as Hants & Dorset – were extremely well detailed and worthy of collection. In the rush-hour it was possible to see an occasional open-top car pressed into service and it is fortunate that one was set aside, complete, before the trams faded away in 1949.

Returning by the same route to Above Bar, with peak traffic in full swing, it might be possible to find an older bus helping out on the 53 service via Botley and Wickham to Fareham. Once this turned out to be TD644 (JT 9353), a Brush-bodied Bristol K5G, which left West Marlands with a full load of standing passengers in the middle of the rush-hour. It grumbled along well enough until Bitterne station, after which it was faced with the fearsome climb up Lances Hill. It was not dual carriageway at that time and any slow-moving vehicle had a knock-on effect on everything behind it and TD644 was very slow! Halfway up the long hill, grinding away in second, the revs began to die and the bus came to a stop. Steam enveloped the front and our driver, after one rueful look, set off to obtain assistance. About ten minutes passed before he returned with a watering can and began to refill the radiator. It took almost three cans of water to refill it. Restarting on Lances Hill with a full load was no joke for a 7 litre diesel and first gear was wisely selected; shuddering under its load, the TD crept away and toiled up the steepest part to the summit at Bullar Road while a great cheer went up from the passengers. We reached Fareham half an hour late!

The 1940s period has a special place in my affections for it covered my earliest personal experiences of transport, when the variety and character must have been second only to that pertaining in the 1920s.

Below: Domed-roof tram No 2 makes its final departure from Portswood depot after abandonment of the last Solent area standard gauge system in 1949. */Southern Newspapers Ltd*

Epoch IV

1949~1959, The Turn of the Tide

17
'The Middy'

To admit that my first contact with railways was through the medium of a tinplate Hornby O-Gauge train set is not, in any way, to deny the 'might, majesty, dominion and power' of the real 12 inches to the foot invention. Rather that my full size experiences were limited to watching an occasional train rumble past my father's allotment near the Western Road at Cosham, or standing on the footbridge at that station while some angry monster roared underneath, enveloping me in smoke and steam. Only very vaguely am I aware now of any numbers or types: flat sided 'spam-can' Bulleid light Pacifics, C1-series austerity goods engines and some tall-funnelled tank engines. There was also a long black locomotive with many wheels used in the Ordnance Depot at Hilsea; as this last type was visible from the front of our house in Military Road (as well as an old saddle-tank loco with a brass dome and a name, now forgotten), I began to take a greater interest in the offspring of Stephenson and Watt. Before the coming of American Servicemen to Hilsea, the land opposite our house had been a field – full of wild blackberries, exciting paths and even a walnut tree. Then came bulldozers and workmen, fencing and huts to spoil the view, but at least they extended the railway across Peronne Road! In a year or two, whilst still at St John's, my curiosity about railways began to get the better of me so that I purchased an Ian Allan ABC booklet of the Great Western Railway – dated 1947 – for the princely sum of 1/6d. Why GWR you may ask? Although it was soon to be followed by a Southern edition of 1946, purchased from a small model shop in Fratton Road, the reason I chose the GWR booklet initially was because I had seen a strange kind of engine at Fratton station. It had a copper-capped chimney and brass safety-valve bonnet with the letters 'GWR' on its tender! In thumbing through those pages I found No 4989 *Cherwell Hall* and reference to one of the War Department engines at Hilsea, No 79301, an 8F 2-8-0 built for the Ministry of Supply as part of the war effort. Unfortunately, I have never been able to trace the old saddle tanker, nor find any photographs of steam locomotives at Hilsea. However, a couple of pictures of WD stock at Longmoor and a wartime view of Eastleigh Yard came to light in the archive collection at *The News*.

For my sins I managed to pass the Eleven-Plus examination and was placed for the start of my senior schooling in September 1948 with Churcher's College at Petersfield. As a 22-mile journey each way per day was out of the question from our new home at Catisfield, I must needs become a boarder; this restriction, which related to three-quarters of each year, was more and more irksome to one who had many interests outside the academic side of

school life but with little inclination towards the usual sports. Nevertheless, once I could aspire to a bicycle the situation became tolerable and my earliest exploits with a camera came to be undertaken after a couple of years there. Furthermore, thanks to the kindly interest of two masters, Mr E. C. Ive and Mr J. Byl, the mysteries of developing and printing monochrome films were unfolded at Camera Club meetings. Initially my special interest remained with buses – the Petersfield species of which I shall touch on in the next chapter – but even on my first eventful day at Churcher's I noticed *The Railway*!

Boarders were given license to descend upon the town after school on Fridays only – subject to the claims of 'detention' if one had transgressed – and on Sunday afternoons from 1.30pm we were cast out upon the unsuspecting countryside to beguile the time at least until 3.30pm but no later than 5 o'clock roll-call. At all other times we were restricted to the school grounds which, thank God, were extensive and pleasant. There was an assault course for members of the Cadet Force, a swimming pool for summer, tennis courts and several

Top: One of the 'Austerity' 2–8–0 locomotives of American design that appeared in Britain during World War II. No 2292 was used for a time on the Longmoor Military Railway – this view of it coupled to old passenger stock is believed to be at Liss Junction about 1943.
/*The News, Portsmouth*

Above: The Great Western in Portsmouth. 4–6–0 No 4989 *Cherwell Hall* heads the 2.45pm train to Reading General at Platform 1 of the Low Level station on 8 April 1957./*Author*

Right: Bird's eye view of Portsmouth & Southsea station from behind the ruined clockface of the Guildhall in the late-1940s./*The News, Portsmouth*

playing fields together with a corner for gardening known as the Plots. It was from this furthest outpost of the school's domains that closest views might be obtained of 'The Middy', that rural railway serving Rogate, Elsted and Midhurst from the main London-Portsmouth direct line at Petersfield. Having noticed its existence – a fact curiously omitted from the list of amenities in the College Prospectus – I became more aware of it on my first Friday visit to the town. In autumn and spring terms school ended at 3.45pm, so that passers-by might observe a veritable torrent of boys pouring out of the gates about this time, their numbers being swelled on Fridays by around a hundred boarders eager to spend their pocket money on such small home comforts as could be bought at all during rationing. My own pocket money amounted to a mere 1/6d per week, of which some was required for stamps on letters home and 1d for church collection each Sunday. As I ran down the slope of Ramshill, filled with a glorious sense of freedom for one brief hour, I heard a rumble and squeal of a tight flange on rail. Before my eyes a goods train trundled across the skew bridge at the foot of the hill, puffing gently by with its handful of wagons towards the junction. I had not thought to bring my ABC Guide up to school, so was no wiser as to its type, but there was no difficulty in remembering the number as it passed. No 30327 was the engine, with a rusty patch near the top of its stove-pipe chimney, running tender-first towards Petersfield with the daily goods returning from Midhurst. Southern enthusiasts will have had no difficulty in recognising it as one of the 30 Drummond 'Black Motor' 700 Class 0-6-0 goods engines inherited from the London & South Western Railway and already 50 years old. Soon I discovered that it could be seen running chimney-first on the outward leg at just after 1.30pm each weekday, a factor that encouraged me to take up gardening, to qualify for one of the plots in that far corner of the grounds. . . .

In ensuing weeks and months I was often to be found leaning on a spade during the break before afternoon school, contemplating not the establishment of a miniature Kew but the magic of a scruffy old Black Motor heading away towards Midhurst with perhaps half a dozen assorted goods wagons. All regular Guildford engines appeared in due course – Nos 30308, 30325/6/7 – as well as an occasional visitor from Feltham. While waiting for the goods it was possible to see a passenger train come in from Midhurst at 1.20pm, since its arrival was a necessary prelude to the passage of another train over the single line. All passenger trains consisted of push-pull carriages, either red or green, coupled to a small tank engine. Almost always this would be chimney-first to Midhurst like the goods train and regularly featured one of the many auto-fitted M7 0-4-4T locomotives also designed by Drummond. In my early days at Churcher's I found Nos 30021, 30056, 30060, 30108-10, 30328 and 30481 taking turns, but a fellow gardener pointed out a different breed of engine during morning school one day – thanks to a pair of binoculars he kept about his person! John Balls came from Lymington and was familiar with M7 tanks on the branch from Brockenhurst, but from our classroom it was not possible to be sure about numbers even with the aid of 'high power'. Fortunately Mr Cottle, our mathematics teacher, was tolerant of transport enthusiasms having owned a variety of interesting cars himself – we were often regaled with tales of his Trojans, when the intricacies of algebra became tedious even for him! As luck would have it this newly-discovered type of tank engine appeared sometimes during the lunch break, with Nos 32364/5 and 32384 being noted from the sanctuary of the Plots (with the aid of those binoculars). As these ex-LBSCR D3 0-4-4T engines were based at Horsham they did not perform all day long, which brought us to the conclusion that certain trains must run through to or from Pulborough. However, by keeping diligent observation of our 'Middy' whenever possible, it was discovered that no through workings by Horsham engines occurred on Sundays. In fact, very few trains ran at all on Sundays and their timings were different. Although we were officially prohibited from Petersfield except on Fridays, the town being declared 'out-of-bounds', it could be argued that it was necessary to go round its edge in order to walk (or cycle) towards Butser, Steep or East Meon. Fortified with such questionable logic, not to say an occasional ice cream from a strategically-placed shop, it was possible to examine the complete train at leisure.

The Midhurst bay was not attached to the main station at Petersfield at all. There was a non-electrified loop platform on the up side that may have been used before regular-interval electric trains caused the level-crossing gates to be closed to road traffic at least six times each hour, but the 'Middy' was to be found at a humble structure across the road, adjoining a dairy. There it would sit on Sunday afternoons, whiling away the time until 3.19pm. An occasional panting sound would come from the Drummond tank as its Westinghouse pump stirred briefly before sinking into a sizzling reverie, while doors stood open on fine days inviting prospective passengers to make themselves comfortable on the faded cushions within.

The timetable said third class only, but several of the old panelled coaches offered first class accommodation also, though I suspect it was seldom used. As there was little chance to capture the thrill of a steam train in action when it would disappear under Tilmore bridge almost at once, we railway enthusiasts used to walk back to Ramshill well prior to departure and wait beside the track at Mugg's Mede crossing, a stile provided to give public access to a foot-path just east of the road bridge. A cheery whistle gave advance warning of the train's approach, to the accompaniment of vigorous puffing uphill by the M7. In typical schoolboy fashion, it was not uncommon for us to place a farthing or old halfpenny coin upon the rails in order to have it enlarged to twice its former size by the passage of the little train; then, with growing hunger for tea, we would stroll along Love Lane to enter the grounds by the back way, a week's freedom extinguished like a snuffed-out candle.

Below: 'The Middy'. An impatient M7 0–4–4T waits to depart with the 7.48am from Petersfield's humble branch platform about 1950./*E. C. Griffith*

18
The Petersfield Connection

Some places seem to be a natural meeting point. Petersfield is such a one, its Square even today acting as a focal point under the noble gaze of its statue of William of Orange on horseback. All around are buildings of period interest: Elizabethan, 17th century, 18th century, proclaiming the town's long association as a place of commerce and culture. As a pupil at one of its schools, I became aware that it was a pleasant place to be living in, although its situation in a fold of the Downs precipitates a goodly proportion of the annual rainfall. This probably accounts for a natural lake formed amidst the Heath (known irreverently locally as 'The Pond'), about half a mile to the east of the main shopping area and a favourite haven for wild duck and other birds. But, while the Heath is still served occasionally by bus, most routes terminate at the railway station to the west of the town.

Being a boarder limited my need of buses mostly to the beginning and end of term, that blessed midway weekend known as half term and times of dire need on Friday or Sunday afternoons. These last occasions might be caused by lingering too long in the shops or being caught without a raincoat when the skies opened – what price a bus when one is puffed-out or wet through? Southdown had a commanding position with two double-deck services to Portsmouth, the 40 via Clanfield and 42 via Horndean. A local service to Cranford Road, dubbed 142, came to be instituted for operation by the bus laying-over before its next working on the 42 – an economical arrangement that found favour with all except its crew, whose tea-break in a café near the station was severely curtailed. East-

Right: Outside Petersfield station, Southdown Leyland Titan TD4 140 (CCD 940) pauses between journeys to Bognor Regis on service 60. Still fitted with its original 52-seat lowbridge Beadle body, this view must date before 1950./*D. Clark*

ward there were two more regular double-deck routes – lowbridge operated – comprising the 60 to Midhurst, Chichester and Bognor and the 61 to Midhurst, Petworth and Horsham. The former ran past the College to Rogate and Trotton while the 61 travelled beside the lake and over the downs to South Harting and Elsted on its way to Midhurst. After withdrawal of Sunday trains on the Midhurst branch due to a coal shortage in the winter of 1951, a short working to Rogate station was introduced for single-deck operation by the 1400-type, numbered 60A, since the station was more than a mile from the village of that name! Two additional services operated on certain days only, both being between Petersfield and Chichester. No 54 served the Heath, South Harting, Compton, Churcher's Corner and Funtington whereas the 62 reached South Harting via Sheet and West Harting, continuing via East Marden and Chilgrove to its terminus at Chichester. Thus in theory it was possible to catch the 60 or 62 services back to school when in urgent need. I should also make mention of one other 'occasional' service from Petersfield, which was subsequently cut back and eventually withdrawn altogether; this was the 35 to

Fareham via Chalton, Clanfield, Hambledon, Denmead, Southwick and Wallington. It was worked first by a little Leyland Cub, then by a 1400 Tiger, but suffered from the same problem that has afflicted all attempts to serve rural communities – not enough passengers to cover the cost of just the fuel, let alone wages of staff and cost of depreciation or repairs.

Most useful to us pupils were the Aldershot & District buses, since all three of its services stopped outside the school. A double-deck Dennis Lance with lowbridge East Lancs body was the staple provision on the 24 between Guildford and Petersfield via Hindhead and Liphook. If one was feeling lazy, it was handy to catch one of these into town on Fridays and to return by it just in time for roll-call. It was often duplicated at peak times to and from Hindhead, numbered 24A. The other two routes were both the preserve of single-deckers, being service 6 between Steep, Petersfield, Bordon,

Below: Just before morning school, with Aldershot & District represented in strength. Strachans-bodied Dennis Lancet J10 No 179 (HOU 905) is on service 6 to Aldershot, while Dennis Falcon 150 (GOU 850) has just arrived from Alton and Selbourne on the 53 route. */Author*

Farnham and Aldershot and the 53 from Alton to Petersfield via Selborne and Liss. In later years lowering of the road under the railway at Wrecclesham enabled the former to be worked by Dennis Loline double-deckers, a Guildford product based on the Bristol Lodekka and built under licence from the Brislington firm. Many day-boys arrived from the Bordon area on the 6, similarly duplicated frequently, particularly at peak periods, despite using 38-seat Dennis Lancet J10 buses from 1950. All the latest single-deckers were tried on this route, including Aldershot & District's solitary Dennis Dominant (174: HOU 900), an underfloor-engined Guy Arab (186: KOU 113) and a hired Dennis Lancet with underfloor engine. All three of these 'one-off' vehicles had full-fronted bodywork, which was still rather eye-catching in the early 1950s. However, as well as this trio, service 6 was given just about every version of the Dennis Lancet created since Adam was a boy, with registrations ranging from AOT to GOU, including a handful with 'coffin' radiators from prewar days. Very occasionally one of these vintage machines would be turned out for the 53 from Alton, but as a rule normal-control Dennis Falcons were used for this pleasantly-rural route.

One other major operator was active in the area with two double-deck routes terminating at Petersfield Square. Hants & Dorset sent its 67 across from Winchester from time to time, serving villages such as Bramdean, West Meon and East Meon with a homely selection of elderly Brush-

Top: Petersfield Square on a Sunday afternoon. Southdown's 40 service from Portsmouth has brought in a rebodied Leyland TD5 249 (GCD 49), while Hants & Dorset offers a choice of 1938 Bristol K5G lowbridge vehicles, both on the Winchester route. 1016 (BTR 306, left) has been rebodied by ECW recently while 1012 (BTR 302) retains its original Brush design, somewhat modified since the war./*Author*

Above: Formerly 174 in the A&D fleet, Dennis Dominant HOU 900 was located at Swaythling in use as a staff bus in 1967./*Author*

bodied Bristols, some with modernised destination layouts in line with postwar Eastern Coachworks examples used on the important two-hourly 50 service from Southampton. Southdown kept an eye on these intruders from the west, having an office in the Square, whilst providing room in their dormy-shed for both H&D and A&D buses arriving late or departing early.

This arrangement continues to the present day, although now the sight of any double-deck buses – apart from Southdown's – must cause the observer to take a second glance. One-man operation has resulted in many changes, apart from normal evolution of design. . . .

In addition to the 'Big Three' mentioned above, Petersfield also played host to some minor operators. One uses the expression 'minor' with some hesitation when referring to Hants & Sussex, although it was really a kind of federation of several areas of operation under one principal, Mr B. S. Williams of Emsworth. A number of stage services commenced from Petersfield but only service 1 (to Liphook via Sheet, Liss and Longmoor) and Town service 5 (to Tilmore Gardens) were operated daily over their complete length. The former was operated with double-deckers such as NCME-bodied Leyland PD1s of postwar construction, but the others were served by an assortment of Bedford OBs with Duple coachwork. Double-deckers were mostly lowbridge, but some outlandish secondhand machines began to make their appearance in the early 1950s – there was a trio from Leicester with the amusing registration ABC and some others I cannot now recall – but traffic to Longmoor Camp was particularly heavy. Bedford OBs included the traditional Vista coaches plus a small batch with attractive bus bodywork featuring curved glass panels in the roof for a better view. On all Hants & Sussex vehicles at this time the colour scheme was a pleasant red and maroon, separated by a cream line or flash. For private hire, in addition to Bedfords in a dual-purpose role, several Leyland Tiger PS1 coaches were available; some were provided with a larger version of the Duple body while the remainder had distinctive Harrington 'Dorsal fin' coachwork. These were often hired by the College for rugby or cricket teams on away fixtures, or perhaps for an occasional music club outing to Winchester or Portsmouth to see some performance of a Gilbert and Sullivan opera. I can recall one especially enjoyable incident when the Headmaster, Mr G. T. Schofield, came along with us and was treated to an impromptu performance of various rugby songs on the homeward leg, with full four-part harmony to boot!

Finally, in my research for this book I came across a nice picture of a Little Wonder bus at Alresford on a stage service to Ropley, Froxfield and Petersfield. Seeing this utility Bedford OWB jogged my memory, for one might be seen in the town on occasion – I believe it was painted brown – the route being by way of Stoner Hill and Little Switzerland, plagued with hairpin bends but very beautiful.

A local firm near the station, George Ewen, also kept a few coaches for private hire during my first couple of years at Petersfield, but these were given up later to concentrate on the haulage side of his business. In summer, however, every Saturday and Sunday a procession of red and green London Transport buses would go through, down to the coast before lunch and back in the evenings about 6.30pm as regular as clockwork. Mostly RTs and RTLs, there might be a green and grey RF or RFW coach interspersed to add to the variety. As the College tennis-court was situated near the main A3 roadway, one could combine a little gentle bus-spotting with an appearance of sporting enthusiasm, a ploy that effectively forestalled critical comment from one's seniors. . . . From the sidelines of the tennis-court might also be seen the whole gamut of coaches proceeding to or from the coast: regular express services, like those of Southdown or Maidstone & District, besides the vast assortment of both prewar and postwar coaches operated by independents like Smiths of Reading or Valliant. More Ian Allan ABC booklets found their way into my possession while a knowledgeable friend, M. G. Button, pointed out the merits of Whitson, Yeates or Dutfield coachwork to my untutored eye. We spent many an hour talking about the passing array of buses and coaches, but I lost touch with him when he left school to do his National Service in the RAF.

19
Last Train to San Fernando

There was a popular song in the 1960s that would have been relevant to British Railways in general and three lines in the south in particular a decade earlier. It went somewhat thus:

'Last train to San Fernando, last train to San Fernando.
If you miss this one you'll never catch another one!
Last train to San Fernando!'

During school holidays I was able to catch up on developments at home for, since my indoctrination into the world of British Railways, I was eager to find more of the myriad steam locomotives shown in my latest ABC. In addition to ticking off their numbers, still a popular pastime with youngsters in this modernised age, I was keen to see some fresh classes and variations to supplement the photographs provided in the book. My chance came on 31 December 1949 when my mother (bless her!) volunteered to take me to Eastleigh for an afternoon of train-spotting. It was intended to be an hour's session on the platform but, after chatting with another boy who was similarly engaged, we decided to see what was visible outside the shed.

The afternoon had started well with a ride to Eastleigh behind Drummond D15 4-4-0 No 30472. Then a trio of engines for the works had been shunted from the shed almost into the platform, giving one a glimpse of a malachite green 'King Arthur' with six-wheel tender and a lined-black 'Schools', while a brace of Z 0-8-0T engines were kept busy in the large marshalling yard. On a pretext of 'just going up the road to see what's outside', my companion and I managed to get off the station without surrendering our tickets, practically tripped over a Guy Arab (CD class) of Hants & Dorset at the entrance and raced along to Campbell Road bridge. Beyond could be seen the vast expanse of Eastleigh Works, not to be visited by me for another five years yet, but towards the south lay the magnetic engine shed, code-named 71A. Several locomotives could be seen outside the north end and more were beside the coaling stage – the place seemed to be teeming with engines of all kinds. After noting all we could see, my companion suddenly tugged my sleeve: 'Look, there's the Leader'. I had heard of this experimental and revolutionary new design by O. V. S. Bulleid, built with a cab at each end and incorporating sleeve valves, but had never seen it before. In the fading light it was scarcely discernible so, on an impulse we entered the hallowed gateway and walked steadily but warily across to examine it further. Whether we were invisible that winter afternoon or whether nobody could be bothered about two young lads fascinated by some scruffy old steamers in the half-

Left: Inside the Works. Major overhauls at Eastleigh entailed occasional visits from far-flung outposts of the Southern empire, as witness Beattie 2–4–0WT No 30586 from Wadebridge in Cornwall on 9 February 1957./*Author*

Below: The 'Leader'. Prototype 0–6–6–0T No 36001 at Brighton on a test train in 1949. Of five engines under construction, only one ever became operational./*National Railway Museum, Crown Copyright*

light I cannot say, but no one bellowed to us and we reached the object of our attention without more ado. Like a great grey slab, No 36001 stood silent and locked – lifeless and alien. We walked round it, little realising that its fate was so soon to be sealed for I never saw it again. Having been successful thus far, it seemed only sensible to walk back past the coaling stage. Flickering oil lamps glowed on each engine, hissing and gurgling as they were coaled up and prepared for their next duties. Not having a watch, I had no idea of time but the red glow in the western sky told its own tale. It was impossible at this juncture to resist having a peep into the shed itself, dimly-lit paradise of Southern steam. Some 'Merchant Navy' Pacifics were there in experimental blue livery, looking absolutely huge in the shadows; there were 'Lord Nelson' 4-6-0s, several 'King Arthur' class variations and so many more it was like a dream. Trying to scribble down numbers in the gloom while recognising strange engines at the same time was no easy matter, for it seemed never ending. . . .

At last I dragged myself away from the wonder of my first shed visit. Leaving its host of engines slumbering in the darkness, I made my way back in haste to the station for I was very late. Hoping to head off the inevitable row, I feverishly planned what to say. Sure enough I got a wigging, but it was worth it! No one could take away that experience of Eastleigh shed and even my mother agreed it had been exciting, when I told her all about it. I had pages of barely-decipherable numbers scribbled down in my notebook to be digested later, for the old Drummond 'Greyhound' No 30287 had brought us back to Fareham already.

In the course of the next few years I accumulated numbers and knowledge while, all around, changes and modernisation were beginning to be seen. The first Standard designs for British Railways started to appear: these were useful 2-6-0s of power Class 4MT numbered in the 76000-series, destined to be the mainstay of Southern steam on our secondary lines for the next decade and a half. Their arrival on Portsmouth-Southampton-Bristol (or Cardiff) duties, working as far as Salisbury before handing over to the Western Region, presaged the departure of the 40-year old D15s as well as other more venerable LSWR 4-4-0s. When No 76005 first caught my attention on a down train from Bristol I little realised how quickly things were going to change – and go on changing! At first the 1948 Nationalisation of all four main railways and several minor ones had seemed an academic exercise, for nothing much seemed to occur. Southern green was gradually replaced by carmine and cream ('blood and custard') on the corridor coaches – after a brief flirtation with 'plum and spilled milk' – while local non-corridor sets and push-pull pairs were either re-

Right: Something of the mystique of Eastleigh shed remained to the end. Light Pacific No 34006 *Bude* sizzles quietly beside a brace of Crompton Type 3 diesels in the final days of steam./*Author*

varnished or painted red all over. Through trains from Cardiff or Bristol still used GWR stock but in time the chocolate lower panels were repainted carmine – hardly a startling change, for there was no mistaking the origin of 'Toplight' carriages! Of course, locomotive numbering was changed (except on the Western) but I had hardly been aware of the old numbers anyway. The solitary T1 0-4-4T locomotive allocated

Below: Fareham teeming with trains. T9 4–4–0 No 30301 arrives with the 11.15am Portsmouth-Bristol through train, composed of GWR stock, while 2MT 2–6–2T No 41317 blows off impatiently with the 11.03am to Andover Junction. 'Black Motor' 0–6–0 No 30316 takes water before venturing out with the Gosport goods on 29 June 1957./*Author* 
Bottom: Successor to the T1 at Fratton, 02 class 0–4–4T No 30207 surmounts the ramp to Portsmouth & Southsea (High Level) station running wrong line in order to curve away into the Dockyard with goods on 8 April 1957. Push-pull gear fitted for use in the West Country was not removed on transfer./*Author*

to Fratton shed (at first coded 71D) was always No 20 and it was withdrawn still bearing those digits. A few engines ran for a year or two with a small 's' prefix to their Southern Railway numbers – D15 No 465 was one of these – but an alternative was to carry the full title 'BRITISH RAILWAYS' on the tender or tank sides. Some repainted engines wore an attractive lined black livery with no insignia at all, an intermediate stage to be found on several M7 tanks working push-pull trains. But no noticeable withdrawals took place until the coming of those early Standards.

The first real jolt to this traditional and orderly state of affairs occurred in June 1953. With regular, frequent bus services provided by Provincial between Fareham and Gosport Ferry, it had seemed rather odd that British Railways ran only two passenger trains each way between the same two towns on weekdays, making an intermediate halt at Fort Brockhurst. It was provided sometimes by the Meon Valley push-pull train, in between journeys to Alton, and at other times by a two or three-coach set of LSWR non-corridor coaches.

At half-term I was able to make a once-for-all trip just a week before closure, with M7 0-4-4T No 30033. It trundled along at a modest pace, having departed from platform 4 at Fareham on the southbound journey. There were no crowds, no camera-toting enthusiasts, to make it especially memorable but just a quiet ride in a third class compartment of a train from the Edwardian era. There was time to look around the dilapidated but historic station at Gosport, much of the former glory of Sir William Tite's design spoiled by a bombing raid in the early war years. Outside was another reminder of its Victorian ancestry; a quaint old postbox inscribed VR, standing in Spring Garden Lane near the gates that would be closed across the road on occasions when wagons had to be moved in or out of the Clarence Yard.

One scarcely missed the passing of Gosport's passenger trains, for the line remained open for goods or parcels traffic and

Above: Inside Gosport signal cabin, the Station Master holds a single-line token and pouch for the section to Fort Brockhurst. After withdrawal of passenger services signalling was simplified and this box closed. /*The News, Portsmouth*

life went on much as before. The real shock came 18 months later when closure was announced of both the Meon Valley and Petersfield - Midhurst - Pulborough branches. In retrospect, I suppose some hint of their fate had come from suspension of Sunday services during the coal shortage in 1950/1– the most strange manifestation that all was not well being the temporary replacement, for about a fortnight, of familiar tank engines on The Middy by an austerity Q1 0-6-0 tender locomotive, which looked rather ridiculous hauling just two ancient push-pull coaches. This arrangement caused all manner of problems at Petersfield because there were no run-round facilities in the official Midhurst bay platform. Run-round had to be performed in the down main platform instead. Departure was also made from there, using an old lower-quadrant home, signal provided at the north end close by the level-crossing gates. Observations noted the use of Nos 33001-33005 and 33014-33016 on these duties, one locomotive being in action throughout the day to eliminate a change over in mid-afternoon, with its consequent light-engine movements to and from Guildford shed, necessary with tank engines due to their smaller coal bunkers. Sunday afternoons were no longer enlivened by the stirring departure of the 3.19pm to Midhurst, itself a way of telling the time, though the coaching-stock stood forlornly in its appointed bay until Monday should come round again. But at the end of November 1954 the dreaded notices began to go up indicating that the line would close – like its fellow between Alton and Fareham – from 7 February 1955. During the last two or three weeks of that autumn term, with rehearsals for the Dramatic Society's production of Shakespeare's *The Tempest* in full swing, there was some relaxation of the usual rules about leaving school grounds for senior boys, which made it possible for me to see more of the train's activities than usual. During a morning walk into town to purchase a gift for the play's producer, Mr W. R. Kershaw, I leaned over Tilmore bridge to watch the arrival of the daily goods – operated since 1952 from Pulborough and Midhurst to Petersfield by a Horsham or Three Bridges engine. Below, E5x 0-6-2T No 32570 drew up at the junction signal to await clearance across the main lines into the goods yard

Below: Petersfield's solitary lower-quadrant starter stood by the level crossing at the northern end of the main Down platform. Four years after closure of the Midhurst branch, Drummond 700 class 0–6–0 No 30350 arrived with the Portsmouth Direct Line Centenarian special train for Gosport on 25 January 1959./*Author*

beyond. Its load was a mere handful of wagons comprising coal and sugarbeet. The engine's well-proportioned lines were set off by clean black paintwork lined-out after the fashion of the London & North Western before Grouping. It struck me that this simple scene, taken for granted during my six years and more at the College, was soon to end – not just for the holidays or at weekends, but for all time. The true significance of this impending farewell to our Middy became clear; it was a sombre moment.

Over the Christmas holiday period I resolved to take a ride upon the little train that had been so much a part of our lives at school. On 29 December 1954, armed with a new camera (but scant knowlege of how to use it correctly!), I travelled up to Petersfield from Fareham station to catch the 10.40am departure for Midhurst. It was a miserable day, cold and wet, so I hurried across the road to the bay after purchasing my ticket with no more than a brief glance to confirm that the engine was an M7, while its train consisted of a mere single carriage built for the 'Brighton' long ago. Perhaps surprisingly, it had an internal corridor along its full length, so that one might choose a clean, cosy compartment with a good view. With a perfunctory whistle and a slight jerk, the 10-mile journey began: when the smoke cleared after Tilmore bridge, energetic sounds began to filter back as the old Drummond tank began to tackle the rising gradient past Pirelli's ITS Rubber factory siding towards Ramshill bridge over the main London road. Then, with another blast of the whistle for Mugg's Mede crossing, guarded from the opposite direction by a fixed distant signal, No 30108 began to gallop along the embankment within sight of the College before entering Durford Wood. It was quite a brisk ride and the four miles or so to Rogate did not take very long. Where once two platforms had been in use at the station for Harting, one now sufficed for a solitary passenger awaiting the diminutive train. Beyond, in the goods yard, several wagons

stood dripping in the steady downpour in anticipation of a freight train later in the day. With much hissing of steam, No 30108 ambled away eastward through the lush green fields and leafless trees of West Sussex downland in winter for a further couple of miles to Elsted. Here there was no one but the railway's general factotum to exchange a word and see us away. The little train gathered speed once more, soon plunging into more woodland to reach its maximum on the curving descent past Midhurst Common – the South Western's original terminus – before slowing beside extensive sidings and a dilapidated engine shed for the disused junction for Chichester. A couple of minutes ahead of schedule, the train stopped in the through platform at Midhurst – an ornate and once-busy station built for the LBSCR in late-Victorian days with all that period's solid virtues. From the shelter of its awning I saw E5x tank No 32576 in the bay, while a whistle from the direction of the tunnel indicated an arrival from Pulborough. Into the westbound platform steamed another push-pull train, also of one coach, which would take me back again if I hurried through the subway.

In less than half an hour I was back in Petersfield, my ride by 'Middy' over, and it was still raining. Although I took two or three pictures of the train, both my inexperience with the camera and the chemist's subsequent carelessness in dealing with my order resulted in a collection of tiny contact-prints and no negatives! How one wishes it was possible to wind back the pages of history and relive it all using a quality camera, never mind the rain. . . . The nearest one is likely to get is an out-of-season visit to the Bluebell Railway when a short train is running with the Chatham 'H' tank, for the station and subway at Horsted Keynes are not unlike the now-vanished platforms of Midhurst. To be truthful, I did manage one further ride on the Middy, but that was on its final public day; both that occasion and the following day's 'Hampshireman' special train deserve attention in the next chapter.

20
The Dentist and the Last Post

Few of us relish visits to the white-coated wizard who pokes about among our teeth with a single-pronged rake and miniature mirror to discover how many warrant drilling, filling or extracting. As I had never opted for the school dentist but resolutely remained loyal to the one at home in Fareham, it just so happened that a couple of fillings needed to be done after Christmas. By special permission – seeing that I was by this time a senior prefect and Deputy House-Captain into the bargain – a dispensation was granted for me to go home on two consecutive Saturday afternoons towards the end of January to visit my dentist. As it was a trifle cold for cycling, in the ordinary way I should have taken either the bus or the train via Cosham. On these two occasions, however, I contrived to catch the Hants & Dorset 67 bus from Petersfield as far as West Meon and complete the journey by train! My credit must have been good with the College kitchen staff, for I managed to cadge a packed lunch in order to save time at the end of morning school. Travelling light (which included my camera) I reached the station by 12.45pm, which allowed me 10 minutes to photograph the Midhurst goods, while it stood ready and waiting behind another freight

train destined for Guildford in the loop platform. On each occasion I was favoured with an E5x 0-6-2T (32576) for my picture, before hurrying across the level-crossing to catch the Winchester bus.

By 1955 the prewar Brush-bodied K5Gs had been scrapped or rebodied, to be replaced by a postwar Bristol double-decker with Eastern Coachworks body. The journey to Langrish is along the A272 – that inland cross-country road that straggles between Stockbridge and Lewes, by-passing the busiest towns – after which the bus takes to narrow lanes through East Meon to West

Right: Meon Valley passenger: M7 0–4–4T No 54 and ex-LSWR push-pull set look hopefully for passengers at Privett station./*Lens of Sutton*

Meon, before setting the passenger down at the 'Thomas Lord'. While the bus turned northward briefly along the A32 to regain the A272 at West Meon 'Hut', I had time to walk on through the village past its lovely thatched cottages, before climbing uphill to match the level of the high girder viaduct that brought the railway south from Alton. Everything was quiet at the station, for only one freight and four passenger trains in each direction used it daily from Monday till Saturday; like the Midhurst branches, whose fate it was to share within a few days, Sunday trains had been suspended since the coal shortage and never re-instated. The signalman-cum-porter pulled off the home signal for an up train and came to issue me with a single ticket to Fareham. Shortly afterwards the goods appeared behind a '700' and, on surrendering the single-line tablet, ran into the up platform to await the arrival of the down passenger train. On the first occasion it was No 30326 while the second produced No 30350, both then Guildford (70C) engines. Once tucked into the loop, the road might be set for the down passenger, due at four minutes to two o'clock. A distant rumbling indicated it had reached the viaduct and was coasting gently into the station, propelling a brace of push-pull carriages in faded red livery. Set No 662 had started life under the old South Eastern & Chatham, but survived to see out the last days of the Meon Valley line coupled to an LSWR M7. Unlike the Middy of my trip a month earlier, this train was well patronised with no chance of a corner seat. It proved to be no sluggard either, since allowing for three intermediate stations and a halt before Fareham with tablet exchanges to be performed, an average speed of 30mph was called for over an entirely single-line route. At Wickham station the down goods had been shunted into a refuge siding, headed by a T9 4-4-0, while the briefest of halts at Knowle enabled a brisk run along the triple-track section before diverging through Funtley Tunnel. An enjoyable ride ended in Platform 1, in ample time for my dental appointment at three o'clock.

Making these farewells to the Meon Valley a week early, I was able to concentrate my whole attention on the Middy's closure. In a way this was far more drastic: at least a skeleton goods service would continue to operate between Fareham and Droxford, while Farringdon was to be worked as a siding from Alton – after the fashion of Treloars – but of 3½-miles length. Both Butts Junction and Knowle would continue in use, but for the nine miles from Petersfield to Midhurst Common not even a thrice-weekly reprieve was offered. Nothing less than total abandonment – and no one had heard of Beeching yet! Wearing my Railway Club Chairman's hat, I asked the Headmaster if a ride on the Middy on its final day might be permitted, a request that was kindly allowed after lunch on Saturday, 5 February 1955. About 30 boarders took advantage of this authorised leave-of-absence, together with a handful of local day-boys and their sisters or girl-friends from the High School. Mr D. Diamond, Senior Science Master, also accompanied us on his first, and last, ride on the local train, which was duly strengthened to three coaches (instead of the customary one or two) for the occasion. Set No 653 plus an additional single auto-coach (of the variety used on my previous journey at the end of December) were headed by No 30028, starting from the loop platform at 2.50pm. Before shepherding Railway Club members to the station to obtain a party booking, there had been time to watch the last goods pass through Mugg's Mede in the care of a Billinton E4, No 32520, a sad spectacle that appeared to pass un-noticed by anyone else that I could see. Because of the extra carriage on the train, our M7 tank could not operate push-pull; indeed, it had been worked into the station bunker first. Running the engine round to its proper position, shunting the stock and opening level-crossing gates on innumerable occasions took up most of the spare time between duties, but at last all was ready for departure.

The big wheel for Petersfield's level-

Left: Meon Valley freight: All is quiet at Droxford as the 10.20am Alton-Fareham pick-up goods trundles in headed by Greyhound T9 4–4–0 No 30726 during the final week of full operation in February 1955. /*The News, Portsmouth*

Below: Last public train from Fareham to Alton (dep 6.48pm) prepares to leave behind Drummond goods 0–6–0 No 30326 of Guildford shed on Saturday, 5 February 1955. /*The News, Portsmouth*

crossing was being turned up in the signal-box and all four gates swung in unison across the A272. Up went the branch semaphore signal on the gantry while the guard checked that doors were closed. With a shrill blast on his whistle, answered by a longer one from No 30028, we steamed majestically out of the station, with some acoustic effects from a few fog detonators to mark the occasion as honour demanded. There was both elation and anger, pleasure yet sadness at the finality of it all. More passengers somehow managed to squeeze on board at both Rogate and Elsted, while after arrival at Midhurst the platform was thronged with people. A few pathetic pictures were taken to record this event for posterity and No 30028 pushed its stock out of the bay once more to run-round before returning home. We stood about in the watery sunshine, finding it difficult to comprehend that our little train was really going to cease – not next year, not sometime in the future, but today! With so many other people at the station it seemed unthinkable this was 'The End' yet, like us, they seemed a bit overcome by it all. One or two had the foresight to buy some old Southern Railway tickets at the booking office – collectors' pieces today – while the train was shunted back into the main platform for our departure for Petersfield. It really seemed such a shame. . . .

Once back there was all the same rigmarole to be carried out again, but the presence of a replacement engine (30027) made matters easier. For the 4.20pm departure there were more crowds jostling to find seats while for us there was a leisurely walk back through the town before tea at five o'clock. We gave a last wave as the train whistled to us at Ramshill bridge and then it was gone, carriage-wheels beating their rhythmic tattoo on each rail-joint in a way that Reverend Audrey describes so well. Goodbye, Middy! Next day would see one final train over our branch, but this was no ordinary service with push-pull stock for local folk. Billed as 'The Hampshireman', it was a Special Excursion organised by the Railway

Left: Under Tilmore bridge, E5x 0–6–2Ts Nos 32576 and 32570 shift the 10-coach 'Hampshireman' special train with some vigour as they enter Petersfield station with the last train ever to run from Midhurst on Sunday, 6 February 1955./*Lens of Sutton*

Correspondence and Travel Society running from London to cover both Midhurst branches and the Meon Valley line on its round trip, with two changes of motive-power en route. As it was Sunday, a large number of boys gathered along the line near Mugg's Mede after lunch to await developments, there being much discussion among the learned fraternity regarding choice of engines and the train's ETA. The sun was surprisingly warm as we stood fidgeting, trying to find a good spot yet able to follow the train quickly when it came. A distant whistle raised our flagging spirits and binoculars were at a premium to catch a glimpse, far off. The long train was coming very slowly, so that it was some little time before we could determine what was at its head. At last it was beyond doubt: double-headed by a brace of sparkling E5x tanks, Nos 32576 and 32570 coupled bunker to bunker, it plodded steadily round the curve past the fixed distant – which was host to several wilder spirits all waving enthusiastically – hauling ten packed corridor coaches complete with headboard, 'Boat/2nd' brakes and cafeteria car. Awe-struck by the solemnity of the occasion, College bugler McCabe played the Last Post as this magnificent train went slowly by. It was not a sight to be forgotten in a lifetime.

Stupidly, I had run out of film and forgotten to replenish it the previous day, so that I could do nothing but watch helplessly before following the train along to the junction. With screeching of brakes the ensemble ground to a halt, unable to get a clear road into the down platform. How I cursed my ill luck at having no film, for such opportunities for several good photographs were never to be repeated! Many years later, I am most grateful to Mr E. C. Griffith of Farnham and Lens of Sutton for allowing me the use of certain pictures taken on this occasion, since they have a very special significance for me. In due course points were set, a home signal was hoisted into the air and both engines let rip as they moved 350 tons into Petersfield station, before being replaced by a pair of Drummond T9 'Greyhounds' for the remainder of the journey. No 30301, having full-width cab without coupling-rod splashers, was coupled ahead of 30732 which gleamed from a fresh coat of paint and burnished copper-piping. The train's special headboard was transferred to the leading engine and both tanks crossed over to the up loop, while the elderly express engines backed down on to their formidable load. There was magic in watching their departure: with clanking connecting-rods and matched exhaust-beats, they made a determined exodus as a prelude to stiffer work on the northern ascent of Butser. But they were of a different world, a main-line breed already famous in the annals of railway history. What of our poor Middy? Who would wake us at 7.30 on the morrow with a cheery whistle, or tell us breakfast was imminent at ten minutes to eight? To me it was not just a train that was gone, but something I had known since my first day at Churcher's – a familiar, friendly way of life that was part of the curriculum. When the two Brighton tanks, No 32570 now leading, puffed slowly and quietly out with just one last sad wailing whistle to acknowledge a few detonators on the curve beyond Tilmore bridge, it marked the end of an era.

21
Topless Interlude and Naval Review

As painful memories of years of wartime conflict were slowly obliterated by the magnitude of the tasks of rebuilding homes and industry, public transport had one last big boom before the family car began inexorably to sap its life-blood. In Southampton the old trams were swept away in an orgy of bus-buying, until the Corporation fleet was almost 100% standardised on Guy Arab vehicles with Gardner diesel engines. In Portsmouth the trolleys took their last leap forward with the purchase of 15 new vehicles of BUT manufacture built with shapely Burlingham bodywork (Nos 301-315), while extensions to the overhead along Copnor Road and Chichester Road were brought into being during the early 1950s to replace certain motor bus services. During this same period other operators were starting to buy their last 'traditional' buses with exposed radiators, open rear-platforms and half-cab bodywork for double-deckers – already full-fronted coaches and single-deck buses with under-floor engines were a reality – and the bus industry was preparing itself for the most radical developments since pneumatic tyres. All this activity encouraged small coachbuilding firms to design new and exciting body-styles to keep up with the giants, who were unable to satisfy demand. It was a bullish period.

To make room for all the new toys, faithful old friends had to go. The last of Southdown's petrol double-deckers, put out to grass on waste land at Hilsea, were sold off or scrapped. No more lowbridge buses were ordered, while highbridge vehicles eroded their last secure spheres of influence. The final 'coughing' of tapered-radiator Tigers was heard on London summer reliefs and 'UF' registrations vanished when autumn leaves turned to gold; full-fronts (with or without a forward-mounted vertical engine) were all the rage and progress had no time for sentiment. The Horndean and Petersfield services, the 'creme de la creme' of Portsmouth's routes, were safely in the hands of two generations of all-Leyland buses, although many rebodied prewar Titans found safe anchorage sharing turns with wartime Guys to Fareham. On the Havant road new PD2s came thick and fast while a handful of Northern Counties Guy Arab Mark III buses were tried on first this route and then that, as though no one knew quite where best to use them. After their first generation of postwar Tiger PS1 coaches, Southdown leapt from slow-changing 7.4 litre models into synchromesh 9.8 litre heavyweight Royal Tigers fitted with Duple, Leyland or Harrington coach-work designs and centre-entrances. On the bus side of the single-deck fleet, more Royal Tigers harked back to the Harrington TS7s as some were equipped with dual-purpose East Lancs coachwork with doors fitted at rear, centre and front (over a period!).

Over at Hants & Dorset, the Tilling-cum-

BTC influence was beginning to bite. Despite a false trail in 1949, when two batches of six non-standard double-deck vehicles were purchased, soon the relentless bulk-buying of Bristol K, KS and KSW buses brought an end to any further flirtations outside the nationalised fold. AEC Regents with 7.7 litre engines and lowbridge NCME bodies were banished to Bournemouth but the all-Leyland PD2 buses with their high-bridge bodies made Southampton-Fawley services their own; neither type was accorded the distinction of a class letter in H&D's old fleet-numbering system for, in a few months, the whole fleet was renumbered in blocks from 500 upwards. After several unusual acquisitions on the single-deck side, as well as coach-bodies built by Dutfield and Portsmouth Aviation, the same relentless pattern began to emerge with orders for ECW-bodied Bristol LS underfloor-engined vehicles. Some perfectly-good half-cab buses and coaches were rebuilt with hideous full-fronts to match the fashionable trend, while Jefferis' Hedge End scrapyard became the last resting-place for some prime specimens from prewar days – an ex-Elliott Brothers AEC 'Q' type amongst them, never operated with new-series fleet-number.

Perhaps because it had never really given up open-toppers, Southdown was first back into the field with summertime seaside buses. One by one the faithful TD1s that had endured Hitler's war under cover of their canvas roofs began to shed them; Hayling became their local place of employment, but they were not allowed to operate loaded over the rickety Langston Bridge. They lorded it on service 46 between Eastoke and Hayling Ferry via Beachlands and the railway station, being the only double-deckers on the Island. But if their peacetime reign was relatively short, they started a fashion that has never ceased to have a seasonal appeal– provided it doesn't rain! At other times, when not required for sun-seeking crowds on Hayling, the open Titans might be found helping out on rush-hour extras as they had for years – or even

Above: Only lightweight single-deck buses were allowed to operate in service over Langstone's venerable toll bridge, which provided employment for prewar Leyland Cubs and Cheetahs as well as a dozen Dennis Falcon saloons. Car 84 (JUF 84) had a 30-seat Dennis body and was delivered in 1949./*D. Clark*

performing on the new 138 service. Instituted in 1948 to link North End with Fareham via Portsdown and Downend along the ridge of the Hill, this attractive route was reduced within a few years to a workers-only status (along with the 138A, which ran from Havant to Fort Southwick). However, before it was thus demoted, I managed to enjoy a couple of journeys over it. The first was soon after its introduction, using a 1400 Tiger, while the second occurred during school holidays in 1950 when open-top Titan No 820 was provided for a run to Cosham from Fareham in fine drizzle! Being the sole passenger, there was no seating problem so I opted for a windy, exhilarating ride upstairs. After two years at boarding school, I missed the simple pleasure of regular trips by petrol TD1 buses and this 138 journey proved to be my last opportunity. The roads were narrower than they are today, but this was compensated for by a lack of traffic; 820 sallied forth from Fareham and across the Wallington river beside the 'Delme Arms'. Soon it turned off the A27 main road to ascend the slope of Portsdown from Downend, a stiff climb up the chalk ridge leading to the summit at Fort Southwick. There was no pause for breath: down into second for a melodious accompaniment from the transmission before some slight easing of the gradient encouraged the use of third until the battle was won. On level ground it was quickly back into top gear and speed rose into the thirties, with the wind tugging at one's hair, while the veteran showed its unabated zest after more than a score of years in service.

It wasn't long before some utility Guys were in command of Hayling's seafront duties, attractively converted by Southdown into a first postwar generation of topless buses; the Titans had gone. The Guys came to be employed on another novelty: with the renumbering of service 40B to 42A, a new route 140 was brought into use running via Catherington to Clanfield, which was extended in due course on summer Sundays only to East Meon. I have often wished it had been possible for me to sample such a ride on an open Guy – Park Royal-bodied examples were chosen initially for decapitation, but later conversions made use of some Northern Counties bodies plus one solitary Weymann design. The Guys gave excellent service, their Gardner diesel engines being capable of both economy and adequate power to shift a full load without hesitation– even if they lacked the old-fashioned petrol hiss and general liveliness of their predecessors. Strangely, I never managed to travel upon a topless Arab and later visits to Hayling were always by car or by steam train.

In Portsmouth itself, the Corporation continued to employ the four surviving single-deck Cheetahs on seafront duties between Clarence Pier and Hayling Ferry. A feature of their Wadham bodywork was the sunroof, but they must have accumulated very small mileages on disposal for they were used only until 1955. The chief cause of their displacement on the seafront was a new lease of life for certain TD4 double-deckers modified to open-top format. One of the English Electric buses was selected for conversion in Coronaton Year, followed by two more in 1954 and the last a year later (Nos 115, 117, 124 and 125); in due course they were renumbered 5-8 respectively, to allow their old numbers to be re-allocated to further deliveries of Leyland PD2 and PD3 buses from 1958 onwards. Few pictures of the Cheetahs have come to light but transport enthusiasts were not slow to be aware of photographic possibilities with their successors. Indeed, as the years went by and these four stalwarts continued to plod up and down along the seafront, they became a legend and attracted considerable interest. Until 1968 they retained full crimson livery, which suited them well. With such museum-pieces dating from 1935, it was inevitable that little stories about them would be told and retold: how their braking was not to be compared with an Atlantean but that adequate retardation might be achieved by pushing-on the handbrake and then stamping on the footbrake – no instances of body-movement from such extreme measures have been reported to my knowledge. . . . I should, perhaps, explain that on most pre-war Leyland buses and all Portsmouth trolley buses the handbrake (or parking brake, as it was sometimes called) was pushed on, having a large round knob for the purpose: to release, the ratchet was held off and the lever drawn back towards the driver. It is still possible to recapture the atmosphere of these early diesel buses during the summer Rally season, for the entire quartet survived to be preserved – No 8 (RV6368) has been acquired by Portsmouth City Museum.

It was coincidental that the new Elizabethan Age should dawn as Hants & Dorset was completing work on its first home-grown open-top bus, assembled at Winchester Road bodyshop in Southampton to the Company's own design. For this experimental machine the chassis of a 1937 Leyland Titan TD4 was selected, registered CRU 701. Formerly A580, it was renumbered 1005 in 1950; this fleet number was retained after rebuilding as a 57-seat open-

decker, using various miscellaneous parts salvaged from prewar Brush bodies and Strachans utilities. It was a strange vehicle in some respects – full-fronted bodywork with open rear platform was not a commonplace combination locally until Provincial had a number of the Guys rebodied by Readings Coachworks at Hilsea a few years later. Painted in striking coach livery of Tilling Cream with green wings and wheels, No 1005 certainly caught the eye – I came across it just once at Fareham bus station during the summer of 1952, when I was amazed to hear the dulcet tones of a Leyland 8.6 litre diesel purring away beneath its hidden bonnet. The vehicle was always recognisable from six similar rebuilds of wartime Bristol Ks (FRU 303-308) by a pronounced 'snout' above its frontal grille. I can only conclude that this must have been necessary to accommodate differences between the Leyland and Bristol chassis, although radiators were lowered in all cases. Some similarity in frontal appearance is discernable in comparisons with a small group of Bristol LL6B (and subsequent LWL6B) coaches delivered in 1950/1 with full-fronted Eastern Coachworks body-

118

work, which became known as 'Brabazons' as they were the first vehicles of eight-foot width. But while Nos 1106-1111 remained in service for many years to come, proto-type 1005 was retired after only one season. Its body was exchanged with the remaining wartime Bristol K6A, FRU 309 (originally TD778, renumbered 1112 in 1950) which retained all the distinguishing features of its predecessor; the prewar Leyland and its utility body (ex-1112) went for scrap. During the winter five more rebuilds were put in hand, using prewar Bristol K5G chassis selected from the 1938 Brush-bodied group. This series could be recognised by their extra standee-windows above the full-drop ones fitted to the lower-deck, after the fashion of some conversions carried out by Brighton, Hove & District on similar-vintage buses. Also, all five 1953 rebuilds (as well as 1112, with its body off the prewar Leyland) kept their original gearbox-casings with 'Brush' engraved thereon. For the sharp-eyed there remained one further difference between the 1952 series and those rebuilt subsequently, for all the FRU-batch had six-bay bodies while the remainder were of five-bay construction. Many other small differences were to be found between individual buses, since each was – in effect – a 'one-off' job. Their connections with the Solent were limited: for the Naval Review by the Queen in Coronation Year all were in service on the 72 route between Gosport, Lee-on-the-Solent and Hill Head, being subsequently dispersed to Bournemouth and Poole for regular summer duties to Sandbanks or be-

tween Bournemouth and Lymington on the seasonal 218. It was many years before I managed to travel on one in service – three were resold in 1964 to Southern Vectis for similar work in the Isle of Wight, while the remainder were gradually withdrawn between 1968 and 1972. The 1938 Bristol chassis were replaced by postwar GLJ-registered K5Gs in 1957/8 with consequent fleet-number changes for the five vehicles involved, but this was merely to take account of anno domini.

Turning to Gosport & Fareham Omnibus Company, the open-top conversion 'bug' was evident here also. The first attempt was made in 1951 using an ex-City of Oxford AEC Regent No 19 (JO 5403), already in its twentieth year. With its original petrol engine replaced by diesel, allied to a pre-selector gearbox, and Brush body decapitated in much the same fashion as with Southdown's utility Guys it made an acceptable innovation. The following year saw similar treatment meted out to unique Bristol K5G, No 54 (ECG 622); here, again, it was found that utility Park Royal bodies made useful conversions into open-top vehicles for three more (on Guy chassis) were adapted soon after.

But whereas Nos 18 and 56 remained top-less to the end, No 60 was later rebodied by Readings with a full-fronted double-deck 'coach-bus' body based on the half-cab design fitted to No 57 in 1953. Although 57 (EHO 869) was rebodied as a double-deck coach by Readings, it was designed to have a detachable roof for possible seasonal use as open-top – no evidence of its actual use in this way has ever come to light, but at least provision was made for it – an early example of 'convertible' bodywork. Another Provincial open-top bus was to be seen in service briefly during the late 1950s, following damage to its upper-deck sustained at Fareham's notorious skew-arch under the railway station. But No 13 (FHO 605), a postwar AEC Regent equipped with traditional Readings body when purhased new in 1947, was soon restored by the local firm to its former state. It should also be mentioned in passing that the ex-Southdown veteran Leyland G7 open-topper (CD 7045) which had remained active until the end of the war was kept in the depot along with all the 'modern' vehicles; it was thought of very highly by the staff, being taken out once a year for the Gosport Carnival. When re-quired to be moved about the premises it was normal practice to pour a cupful of petrol into the carburettor and swing the huge starting-handle until it fired. It was this regular procedure that ensured its rescue at the time of the dreadful fire in 1957, when a number of buses were damaged or destroyed.

The 1950s were a good example of inventiveness, of carefree, simple pleasures amid the sun and sea-breezes in a popular holiday area; a period when open vehicles survived the change from 'basic' bus to 'fun' bus.

Below: Continuing the topless theme, Southampton Corporation converted two 1946 Guy Arab Mk II buses and painted them in a special livery for summer seasonal work in 1955. No 33 (DTR 460) and 35 were replaced by a couple of Mk III models in 1967. A host of normal Guys and a single-deck Leyland Cub can also be spied at Portswood depot./*Southern Newspapers Ltd*

22
'All Change, Please!'

Few of us are totally satisfied with our lot. Nearly everyone would like to alter some aspect of his present life, but the price of change is that it can never be in complete isolation. As schooldays drew to a close in the summer of 1955 I was impatient to be off, 13 years of education that had began during the war having reached its climax with the new General Certificate of Education 'A' level examination and the chance of a place at university. While awaiting the outcome of some important exams, I left school a couple of weeks before the end of term to begin working to earn some money. At half-term I had been to Hoeford Garage to see Mr H. Orme White – who enjoyed at Gosport & Fareham Omnibus Company virtually the same status as my grandfather had done 30 years before – with a view to being employed for a few weeks of the summer in some useful capacity. With staff on holiday it was always a good time to find

Below: South Parade Pier in all its glory – a view taken about 1946. Behind Southdown's utility Guy 410 (GUF 70) on service 45 to Fareham via Castle Street are two Park Royal-bodied Leyland TD5s and a brand-new PD1 on the 40 route to Clanfield. On the left of this interesting picture is an old Corporation bus-stop sign and a Craven-bodied TD4 heading for Copnor. /*The News, Portsmouth*

casual employment, so it was agreed I would be given a job as a conductor provided the firm's doctor was satisfied I was physically fit. It was necessary to obtain a green badge from the Traffic Commissioners by declaring, amongst other things, that one was cleanly in one's person and fit to be employed as a public servant in a position of trust. With these formalities completed and many hours of examination papers behind me, I carried my belongings from school in both hands and strode purposefully out through the gates into the wide world. . . .

Under the silent, rusting metals of the Middy at Ramshill bridge I had an hour's dalliance to share with my schoolgirl sweetheart, Diana, before the journey by bus home from College for the last time – there was plenty to ponder on, as I took my seat upstairs on one of the all-Leyland Titan PD2s that had been a feature of Southdown's Portsmouth-Petersfield routes since 1948. In my days as a junior, sitting behind the driver downstairs, I had seen some of the JCD-registered buses fitted with a notice about synchromesh gears. Though I didn't appreciate its full significance at the time, it was noticeably absent from earlier postwar GUF or HCD-registered PD1 buses – even from 297 (HCD 897), Portsmouth's earliest all-Leyland bus and especially favoured, as witness its unique chromed bulkhead heater vents! For while all PD1s were pedantic and ponderous between the gears, a singularly brisk acceleration and hill-climbing energy marked out the giant-engined PD2s. Southdown must have been impressed, too, for it bought no less than 192 of them (193, if one counts the Northern Counties coach-bus No 700) between 1948 and 1957, to be followed by a massive total of 285 of the longer full-fronted PD3 series during the next decade. All were powered by the legendary Leyland 0.600 six-cylinder diesel engine of 9.8 litres capacity while a similar underfloor version was employed in the Company's Royal Tigers and Leopards during the same period: it was a formidable vote of confi-

dence at a time when there was more healthy competition in the passenger transport industry than is the case today. Certainly, to me as a bus enthusiast of more than 10 years' standing at that time, the ascent of Butser to Cannonball Corner and on again up to Hogs Lodge was most impressive. The few journeys I had made over the years in those other JCD-registered double-deckers – the Northern Counties-bodied Guys numbered from 500 to 511 (JCD 500-511) – were pretty convincing as well, but slightly more restrained due to Gardner's strict governing of their engines to 1,700rpm. I was to get much closer acquainted with Guy Arabs and Gardner diesels in succeeding weeks. . . .

One of the pleasures of being interested in transport is the wide measure of common ground one finds with other enthusiasts and employees of various companies. My own brief experiences during the few weeks at Hoeford have made it easy to 'relate' to others who have been full-time conductors or drivers. Some have been employed by several companies; their tales of particular incidents or different methods of working are the very essence of one's hobby. There would be a driver who could not abide the bell being rung unnecessarily, for whom a mere tap on the window or stamp on the floor above would be adequate notice to restart. There was a Southdown conductor, usually on the Fareham road, who could imitate bird-calls in a most lifelike manner and frequently would enquire of all and sundry 'Anyone want to pay twice?'. Nowadays, sad to tell, conductors are a dying breed; almost everywhere they have been displaced by the driver/conductor of an OMO (one-man operated) bus, who would have precious little chance to talk or gossip even if he had the inclination. When training on Provincial, I found numerous instances where early-morning passengers knew not only the fare but even the fare-stage number to be used for the old TIM tickets. It may have been through habit, since that company was the last in Britain to offer a 1d adult fare as late as 1955! Yet another nice thing about crew-operated buses was the help a conductor could be to strangers or the elderly. The tale is told of a Corporation conductor who would reel-off every stop, no matter how busy he was or how full the bus; his nasal pronunciation of Ophir Road was particularly memorable. Conductor's tales are very revealing; Peter Tame, who has worked for all the major local bus companies and now helps with British Rail's travel enquiries in Portsmouth, remembers some amusing incidents. Though I do not have his special gift for telling an amusing story, I shall try and relate some of his more memorable anecdotes which occurred during the early 1950s.

Appropriately, his first experiences were also with Gosport & Fareham! It was in the spring of 1950, when there was a home match at Fratton Park one Saturday afternoon, that Provincial provided several spare buses as a sort of football 'convoy' for such an occasion. On this particular Saturday, their arrival at the Ferry was far from routine: one of the 'men from the Ministry' was undertaking a spot-check and ordered the buses to park by Camper & Nicholson's yard, where six were promptly taken off the road by having their licenses confiscated. In these circumstances it was necessary for the unfortunate double-deckers to be towed back to Hoeford for attention, while the coach fleet – fully booked for a children's outing to the New Forest next day – had to be called upon to deputise for them on service. In order not to fail in providing its timetabled services on Sunday it was necessary for Provincial to farm-out the private hire work to Hutfield's Coaches, while their own vehicles bore fabricated cardboard route-numbers – none was normally necessary for coaches! A hazard of a rather different nature was encountered sometimes while working service 12 to Haslar via Park Road. The usual route was along Alver Road but, if there was a high tide running, flooding might occur. What constituted 'flooding' in Provincial's rule book was if the waters should rise above the

first step on its AEC Regals, in which case diversion via Tescombe Avenue was in order. At a later date this service was cut back to terminate at Park Hotel, an eight minute journey with a two minute lay-over at either end; during an eight hour turn of duty it involved 24 return trips with a maximum fare of 1½d! One last tale of this fleet involves its provision of route numbers on double-deck buses: after the fashion of some London vehicles, a number-box was provided beneath the half-cab canopy externally together with a handle for its operation. An interior box was fitted facing out of the window adjoining the platform on the nearside, equipped with a couple of radio-knobs instead of gearing. With some rationalisation of evening duties, buses used to work routes 1 and 13 alternately or 3 and 14 – as you can imagine, the conscientious conductor would spend much of his time changing route numbers in either direction, but this practice rapidly fell into disuse unless an Inspector was reported to be in the vicinity. . . .

Below: A Hutfield's vehicle on stage-carriage work: Driver Cyril Fletcher stands beside his Guy Vixen GOU 593 before working to Grange Estate via Stoke Road, a service taken over by Provincial in 1950. */R. Brown collection*

Peter Tame moved on in due course to work for Portsmouth Corporation where he found there was an excellent training-scheme for new recruits. The three-week course began with two days in 'school', followed by more than two weeks' route-learning spread over both buses and trolley buses. Finally, an inspector would take out a class of about six collecting fares, passing out on the third Friday. His own first solo experience with a trolley bus was rather dramatic. His mate was newly-qualified – so far as driving trolleys was concerned – and the weather was characteristically wet. Their first trip on service 3 from Cosham railway station to South Parade Pier via Fawcett Road was without incident until they reached the Strand. In order to turn left from Waverley Road towards South Parade, it was necessary to operate the frog for the overhead wires by hand; as Peter pulled it in during the downpour and blew his whistle for the driver to proceed, when the bus began to move he got a 'kick' from the handle which caused him to release it prematurely. As one can imagine, off came the poles; swinging round violently, they broke the insulators on the 'coupling' to the wires! If this was an inauspicious debut with trolleys, subsequent adventures were no less hair-raising. Each summer a firework display was given at the Canoe Lake on Wednesday nights, bringing many extra passengers to South Parade Pier – without many private cars, additional buses were the mainstay in taking people home. One Wednesday night, having loaded up adjacent to the Pier, his trolley was creeping forward to turn right into Clarendon Road but was hampered by all the crowds of people and other vehicles. As luck would have it, a pole became de-wired; such was the crush that it was impossible to withdraw the long bamboo pole from beneath the rear platform in order to remedy this situation. At last, a policeman had to hold back the traffic, while the bus edged forward on battery-power far enough to enable the bamboo to be drawn free to re-wire the errant pole! But if motorists were sometimes caught out by the trolleys' powers of

Below: At North End during the 1940s can be seen Craven-bodied 232 (RV 8314) and 217 with English Electric bodywork (RV 6375). A grey-painted Southdown TD1 has stopped at the junction, bound for Fratton Bridge on a pre-rushhour journey.
/The News, Portsmouth

acceleration after a stop – especially with the powerful BUT-series, on which it was sensible to lean well forward after ringing the bell, to compensate for its G-force – quite the opposite might occur with one of the early experimental buses. On one Dockyard Special, an un-numbered service to Cosham via Alexandra Park at the height of the rush-hour, Sunbeam 210 was turning left from Park Road across Guildhall Square when it came to a dead stand on the frog for Blackfriars Road. Being without batteries, the wretched vehicle was bereft of all power right in the busiest part of the road. . . . The day was saved by its bus-load of Dockyard 'mateys', who got off and pushed the luckless machine clear of the dead-section!

A couple of years between 1952-1954 followed with Hants & Dorset, allowing much greater variety of route operation due to its country services, before Peter had a spell with Southdown. He nearly got a job with Hants & Sussex as a conductor on the 14 service, operated between Fareham Market and Catisfield using lowbridge Leyland PD1 double-deckers or even a couple of ex-London Transport Chiswick-built lowbridge STLs, but in 1954 this service ceased and its licence was taken over by Gosport & Fareham Omnibus Company – which at once proceeded to provide highbridge AEC Regents, newly rebodied at Readings. Indeed, during my own brief spell as a conductor at Hoeford, the 20-year old No 34 (BOR 766) was a regular performer throughout the day. My sole contact with this service – renumbered 17 by Provincial – was on the first Friday, when I was still learning the various routes. Its crew was an all-female affair, as I discovered to my surprise on arrival at the depot one glorious July morning at 4.50am. The early sunshine and soothing engine-note of that fine old Regent was so soporific that I quietly nodded-off on its inaugural journey out to Catisfield Post Office! It was not until the bus shuddered slightly, when being reversed uphill while turning round, that I feigned instant wakefulness. I need not have worried, however, for there were no passengers at that unseemly hour!

Below: Hants & Sussex service 14 travelled outward via Trinity Street to Catisfield, returning via North Hill to Fareham Market. A lowbridge NCME-bodied Leyland PD1 (LO 52; FCG 523) waits at the foot of High Street before turning right into West Street about 1950. */Robert F. Mack*

23
1957~The Year of the Green Snakes

Seven fateful years after Nationalisation, a Modernisation Plan was produced for British Railways. It hinted at trimming certain uneconomic lines, inaugurating a steady programme of replacing steam by cleaner diesel and electric traction, more integration of a system that was 'British' in name only, for with six Regions to replace four major independent railways it was not surprising that old practices born of separate development continued. The new Standard engines under the seal of R. A. Riddles were mostly an amalgam of the best features of previous designs and, in some instances, were practically straight copies. A few radical or experimental features crept in, such as 10 Crosti-boilered versions of the Class 9 freight engine or limited numbers of Standard 5s being fitted with Caprotti valve-gear in place of the normal Walschaerts. The basic problem with the initial BR steam locomotive programme was that it was not allowed to run its full course before being labelled obsolete, to be followed by many untried diesel designs of marginal benefit. But if some early diesels were far from satisfactory, the extensive provision of diesel multiple-units on cross-country or secondary duties was more successful. The proof of this is seen 20 years after, when many are still in service on all Regions, yet the Southern managed to extrapolate a unique series of diesel-electric powered sets that have proved to be the most efficient (if arguably the least attractive) of the lot.

Eastleigh's DEMU building-programme was divided into two main parts: the narrow-profile six-car units for Hastings line services, which will not be described in detail in this volume, and the local 'Hampshire' two-car sets for regular-interval services between Portsmouth, Southampton and Salisbury and other local duties on non-electrified routes radiating from Eastleigh. Younger readers may be tempted to raise their eyebrows at my mention of two-car units for Hampshire duties, since all but two normally used in the area today comprise three coaches – the exceptions being sets

Nos 1121/1122. The reason is simply that they entered service in mid-1957 with just the two driving-trailers – one containing the diesel generator, guard's compartment with luggage facility and some second class passenger accommodation, while the other included both first and second class seating and toilets. Later, when the new trains had proved themselves by increasing traffic dramatically, it became necessary to add an all-second centre trailer to avoid the discomfort of standing loads. However, before moving on to these developments, it is worth while considering the position immediately prior to their introduction.

A glance at Bradshaw or one of the Southern's own pre-1957 publications will show a number of summer seasonal through trains plus a small group of regular cross-country services provided all the year round with hardly any local services at all. Compared to the twice-hourly slow trains from Portsmouth to Waterloo (plus one fast service) or two services hourly along the coast to Brighton, the Fareham-Netley-Southampton or Fareham-Eastleigh-Romsey services were very sparse. In fact, it was permitted to travel by Southampton train to St Denys Junction and change for Eastleigh when no direct service was available; I have also managed to travel to Southampton Terminus from Fareham via Eastleigh when no train was scheduled via Netley. Some useful oddities did exist, however, such as a through train to Bournemouth from Fareham departing at 1.29pm, or the 8.50am from Portsmouth & Southsea to Winchester City – the latter was particularly handy when I was a law student needing to attend the Assizes, which were held quarterly at The Castle for the whole of Hampshire. Some rather surprising tank-engine turns between Andover Junction and Portsmouth were provided, stopping at all stations using ex-LSWR three-coach noncorridor sets on a pedestrian journey taking more than two hours. Curiously, Sunday services were not much worse than their weekly counterparts. Certainly, there was nothing like an hourly service over either route – two-hourly would be more like it –

Below left: Avoiding the double-track 1 in 100 gradient, two-coach Hampshire diesel-electric multiple-unit No 1115 leaves Fareham with the 10.45am Portsmouth-Eastleigh service calling at Knowle Halt, for which the driver collects the single-line 'tablet' on 15 March 1958. /Author

Below: Part of Tite's original design for Fareham station may be seen as Brighton-built Fairburn 4MT 2–6–4T No 42095 pauses with the 8.32am Romsey-Portsmouth via Eastleigh train on 8 June 1957. The engine is running-in from Eastleigh before returning to Ashford in Kent, following overhaul. /Author

and regular-interval timings were a sheer coincidence!

The coming of two-coach diesel sets was not as dramatic as might have been supposed. From the start of the summer time-table in June 1957 certain services were operated by the new trains, but to existing steam schedules to allow for possible teething troubles. Regular travellers had to accustom themselves – as their fellows on electrified services to London or Brighton had done for many years – to look out for headcode numerals, for there was little to distinguish the new diesel units from modern EMU suburban stock (themselves seen occasionally coupled to traditional 2-BIL or 2-HAL sets at peak periods, even as far south as Portsmouth). While head-codes 7 or 57 had become accepted as the trademark of Waterloo-line slows and 60 or 62 passed for Brighton line services (aug-mented by the periodic 15 to Chichester only), semi-fast DEMUs to Southampton Central and Salisbury became 85 while all-stations locals to Southampton only were 43. Eastleigh, Romsey and all stations to Andover Junction were 67, with shorter journeys to Eastleigh or Romsey only scheduled as 65 – but there were problems! With an initial programme of 22 units, numbered 1101-1122, the 'Hampshire Diesels' were not sufficiently numerous to cope with all exigencies. For example, whereas most local steam trains had com-prised a traditional Southern 3-coach set – two Brake/3rds and a 1st/3rd composite, whether corridor or non-corridor – the new sets were less commodious both for passen-gers and their luggage. It was necessary to resort to coupling two two-car sets to cope with Portsmouth-Salisbury semi-fast traffic before long and peak traffic caused even more congestion. In order to manage, it was necessary to cut back modernisation on the Andover line to make good deficiencies on the potentially more-profitable sections, so that British Railways' much-heralded 'end of steam' was far from being in sight. Until a month after the commencement of the winter timetable, most Andover trains were

Above: A slight mishap at Canal Walk, Portsmouth. M7 0–4–4T No 30039 has been unduly energetic with carriage-shunting duties and demolished the headshunt buffer. E4 0–6–2T No 32495 has been called upon to bring assistance (and the breakdown train) from Fratton./*The News, Portsmouth*

Above right: On a bright autumn morning, H2 4–4–2 No 32421 *South Foreland* curves across the Hamble River at Bursledon with the 9.40am Brighton-Bournemouth train in 1955./*Author*

still hauled by superannuated Drummond 4-4-0s or by Maunsell two-cylinder 'Moguls' and some brisk running was experienced in their final weeks on these local services.

Apart from a lack of passenger accom-modation, the newcomers quickly earned the nickname of 'Wailing Whinnies', owing to their whining transmission. Local news-papers soon carried frequent letters of com-plaint regarding noise and fumes, although the winter timetable was a revolution so far as density of service and regular-interval facilities were concerned. It soon became clear to the authorities that something would have to be done both concerning the modest seating capacity and the penetrating exhaust-note. These two difficulties were tackled by building an additional centre coach for all but four of the sets (those numbered 1119-1122 remaining as two-car units) and up-rating the diesel engines to 600hp, but with a silencer incorporated. In this form all the original units continued to operate quite successfully, though their

spartan appearance and creature-comforts have never endeared them to longer-distance passengers. Also, riding in the driving-trailer containing the diesel engine could provide an uncomfortable journey due to vibration and transmission-noise. But if these new-fangled trains were here to stay, there did not seem to be any lack of duties for steam engines to undertake! Because of the reduced luggage capacity, extra van-trains were run to cope with mail and newspaper traffic – an ideal source of employment for more-venerable locomotives – while freight trains were completely unaffected by the new craze. Also, as the diesels were essentially for short-haul passenger traffic, long-distance trains running between Portsmouth and Bristol or from Brighton through to Bournemouth, Cardiff or Plymouth, were hardly altered at all. In fact, the hoped-for increase in local traffic began to rub off on cross-country trains as well. Also, because of the relatively-small fleet of DEMUs, additional summer seasonal trains on Saturdays and at other times were scheduled for steam haulage, so that there was occasionally an increase in the need for traditional locomotives. Nor did it have an adverse effect on the main-line services between Waterloo and Bournemouth through Southampton: these were an entirely different source of traffic and remained loyal to steam-haulage until the end, as we shall see in the final Epoch

covered by this book. Some local trains came to be worked by diesel multiple-units between Southampton and Bournemouth, while Mid-Hants services were handed over to the new form of traction in place of steam push-pull trains between Alton, Winchester City, Eastleigh and Southampton.

The whole edifice was rather precarious and there was little margin for error. On Winchester City-Alresford-Alton services it was found that timekeeping was seriously affected if wind and weather combined to impede progress 'over the Alps', hence the purpose of keeping some two-car units for regular employment on Mid-Hants duties to avoid overloading. After the first year of full use on all the Hampshire lines for which the DEMU revolution had been intended, maintenance needs kept the available fleet rather short with the result that it was found necessary to replace diesel with steam on a few services throughout the winter of 1958/9. The Andover line was chosen once again, since services north of Romsey tended to be lightly loaded in any case. This resulted in one sight that had never been commonplace in the Portsmouth area since before electrification – the use of a steam push-pull train! The journey concerned was operated on Saturdays only, being the 10.39am down from Andover Junction and 12.54pm return from Portsmouth and Southsea. An M7 0-4-4T would propel an elderly non-corridor two-coach set down to Portsmouth and haul it back chimney-first – a truly remarkable sight after all the talk of modernisation! Since the schedules had been slightly accelerated to suit the new image, the old push-pull entourage had to thrash along to keep to time. I was lucky to find out about it before the service reverted to diesel and was able to see both Nos 30125 and 30028 performing near Fareham on successive Saturdays. In the first instance the set used was No 35, made up of a brace of ex-LSWR non-corridor vehicles adapted for motor-train working: the weather was frosty and a sprinkling of snow covered the wooden sleepers on the 1 in 100 gradient of double-track out of Fareham towards Eastleigh. Since 1955 I had been granted lineside photographic facilities by the Southern Region and this privilege was invaluable at such times. I was able to capture on film the sight of this vintage train as it thrust smoke and steam skyward in the crisp, clear air on the ascent beneath Highlands Road bridge and again, after it had passed me, in the cutting. A few weeks later, the weather having become somewhat warmer, I was amused to see No 30028 hauling a couple of ex-LMS corridor coaches that had no earthly resemblance to Southern push-pull– I can only assume that the locomotive (a survivor from my Middy days) had outlived its 'period' train. Future displacements by steam on Andover trains were the prerogative of U Class 2-6-0s, but the whole line was to disappear before much longer: first came the closure between Romsey and Andover Junction (both stations excluded), then Chandlers Ford closed between Romsey and Eastleigh and the line singled, to be followed ultimately by singling of the track south of Botley to Fareham and lifting of the double-track 'avoiding' line round Funtley Tunnel. I shall return to this particular section of track again during the final Epoch.

Perhaps one of the more extreme acts that can be inflicted upon a railway may be instanced by the lamented Midhurst branch. Just as I have dwelt at some length on its final years, so after closure and eventual lifting of the rails by contractors one last indignity had to be suffered. The solid old Ramshill bridge, scourge of many a large vehicle descending the slope at speed, was under sentence. It was demolished during March 1959, four years after the last train had crossed, opening up the road to bigger vehicles and taller buses. Later still, a one-way system was brought into use after some of the embankment had been flattened by bulldozers. Yet, hidden beneath a tangle of bramble and wild flowers, the erstwhile crossing – the stile at Mugg's Mede – must lie mouldering where the remainder of that proud embankment leads away eastward. . . .

Epoch V

1959~1969, Downhill All The Way

24
Trolley Valete

As a Portsmuthian, born and bred immediately preceding World War II, I was so familiar with the crimson and white electric buses with their curious trolley-poles that it was not until their latter days that I realised just how special they were. Life, of course, is often thus! How many of us must secretly admit that we have not truly appreciated something until it has been taken away – or nearly taken away – from us. . . .

It must be admitted that I can't recall those halcyon days when trolley buses were brand-new, with white roofs and gleaming paintwork, fully lined-out and duplicating motor bus fleet numbers between 1 and 100. That Portsmouth's trolleys DID look like that is beyond question, as some of the earlier photographs clearly show, but my youthful experience of them was during the years of rationing, of hardship, of war. At that time they were dull and drab, from design or neglect I knew not, but their dreary grey roofs seemed to summarise the whole picture of the war period. Inside the dim lights at night helped to improve their image, giving them an almost magical quality. The early experimental designs I never came across till later, for they were all stored until the outcome of this conflict was beyond question. A couple of the second series (comprising nine AEC 661Ts with English Electric bodywork) were put back into service towards the end of 1942, but it was the Craven-bodied trolleys with which I was most familiar. As built, the 76 representatives of this type had half-drop front windows on the upper-deck, although anyone bold enough to risk opening one in our kind of weather was likely to get a rough reception from the grown-up, tobacco-addicted passengers who considered that saloon to be their private domain! During postwar reconditioning the front windows were permanently sealed, a development in acute contrast to experiences with certain Bristol Lodekkas and some of Southdown's full-fronted PD3 buses, where opening ventilators had to be 'borrowed' from other better-equipped vehicles to improve passenger comfort on the rare hot summer day.

Night was the trolleys' special time. Right at the end of the war, when bombing by the Germans was becoming limited to an occasional 'V' rocket, I went to my first pantomime at the King's Theatre in Albert Road, Portsmouth, on Boxing Day 1944. After all the excitement of its first act, I followed the course of events for a while with lowered eyelids to be restored to full vigour in time for the final curtain. Emerging into the chill December night with wartime darkened streets, a whole string of trolleys was lined up quietly in the gloom ready to take the revellers home. There was no heating, of course, but it was much warmer than standing on the steps of the King's and, in due time, a sort of warmth grew from the very proximity of a full load of 60 passengers. As the bus stood for the signal to depart, there was a distinct humming – a sound I can recall quite well but which is difficult to describe for the benefit of anyone who may never have heard it. To my childish mind it seemed like midnight when the welcome bell-signal was given and, with a gentle drone, the bus took everyone home. Inside, the dim glow of the shrouded lights was friendly and cosy; outside all was cold and black as Stygian night.

When peace came in 1945 there was general rejoicing. All the old black-out material was torn down and put in the street to make a great bonfire, while effigies of the defeated leaders were put on top to be immolated in due course. Our local bonfire was in Firgrove Crescent and later, much later, we were invited to join the Webb family in their house just behind the Southdown bus garage at Hilsea. At some time in the long evening everyone went out to take a walk and it was during this period that we saw an illuminated bus drive past towards Cosham – it was the preserved vintage Thornycroft! Soon strange trolleys began to appear on Portsmouth's streets, for gradually all (bar one, No 212) of the early examples began to filter back into traffic. As I had never known them by their original fleet numbers, I shall refer to them as they were after the 1938 renumbering. Having been out of action for several years, all these ancient buses had to be overhauled and repainted, with the result that one's first reaction on seeing them was both amazement and delight at their appearance. After the dinginess of those faithful AEC Cravens, the bright antiquity of the assorted veterans was a pleasure indeed. Sitting behind the driver on those faded cushions, I can remember being fascinated by their two-pedal control and glowing circuit-light. When negotiating overhead crossings, points or circuit-breakers, the light would be briefly extinguished with a loud 'click' in time with the scraping of the poles. Generally speaking, only their acceleration was brisk on Pompey trolleys for I can never recall high road speeds with any

prewar examples, though a steady 30 or so might be achieved along London Road or Northern Parade.

Certain features stand out in my mind about the trolleys. At a time when all normal motor buses were half-cab, there seemed something vast about the full-fronted trolley bus; the Cravens were especially roomy, inside as well as out, since the Corporation limited their seating to 52. There was space to stretch out in comfort, in total contrast to the lack of knee-room on a Provincial double-decker, which packed in 56! The high-water mark of electric traction was in 1950, when practically all one hundred prewar trolleys were in service being joined in the final weeks of that year by the new Burlingham-bodied BUT series numbered 301-315. Inevitably I had my favourites. While the new trolleys were much quicker – there were many complaints by members of the public at their abrupt acceleration and deceleration characteristics – I had grown up with the older AECs and expressed my conservatism from an early age. No 300, last of the prewar buses to be built, was always looked on with favour and it managed to linger until the last weeks of trolley operation in 1963. Soon after the entry into service of the BUT series, most of the early trolleys were withdrawn – few survived 1951 and all but two had gone by the mid-1950s. The survivors included 201 (RV 4649), the Daddy of them all, and 224 (RV 6382); 204 had been retained for special occasions as an illuminated bus after its official service days came to an end during 1951 but, following a spell of activity to mark the Queen's Coronation in 1953, it had little further use and was scrapped in 1956. Whilst I was articled to a solicitor in the City during the period 1955-1962 I saw many changes occurring – still unable to credit what was going on before my very eyes, I took hardly any photographs of Portsmouth trolleys, despite the availability of an excellent Zeiss camera (at last!). One classic picture I did manage to achieve in 1958: it was the last year that the two veteran AECs were in use and either or

Above: While the little newsagent on the corner of Lucknow Street, by Fratton Bridge, is no more, thanks to redevelopment policies in Portsmouth, this picture recalls the scene as it was after World War II. First of the trolleys, AEC 661T No 201 (RV 4649), was still active on summer reliefs until 1958, found working on service 3/4 on 26 August./*Author*

both might be found working short journeys between North End and South Parade Pier on services 3/4 throughout the day during the summer. One lunch-hour I went to the model shop in Fratton Road – where the original ABC booklets had been purchased more than a decade earlier – and spotted 201 coming over Fratton Bridge as I came out into the street. It was a dull day which enabled me to record it against the light whilst it was working towards North End on service 4. A few days later on a sunny August evening, I managed to pro-

cure a ride on it from the Dockyard. It was a lucky chance, for it was withdrawn and de-licensed at the end of that same month, along with 224. However, unlike that vehicle, 201 was stored away at the back of Eastney Depot until it was found a home at Beaulieu, to be displayed at Lord Montagu's Motor Museum.

This is not the place to narrate the sad tale of friction that marked the final years of trolley operation in the City. Despite trials in 1955 with a new Sunbeam trolley bus from Walsall, the Suez crisis and subsequent fuel rationing in 1956/7, no further trolleys were purchased for Portsmouth and a campaign was mounted gradually to abandon them in favour of motor buses. It is easy to say, now, that the City Council was wrong! There was much opposition to its decision to abandon at the time, but all the indications were that it was justified on economic grounds and was supported by a firm of business consultants. Trolley buses were gradually abandoned and replaced either by re-routing of existing motor buses – such as Southdown's 45A service to replace the 13/14 trolleys through Victoria Road South – or by the provision of new vehicles such as Metro-Cammell Weymann-bodied Leyland Titans (of both PD2 and PD3 variants), culminating in a new breed of rear-engined motor bus for the 'coup de grace'. Being away at law school in London during 1960/1, I did not see much of their declining years but I was back in time to record the passing scene of three trolley-routes terminating at the Dockyard. The end came during the summer of 1963; on 22 June services 17/18 were worked for the last time by trolleys, marking the final appearance of prewar Craven - bodied vehicles on the streets of Portsmouth, while the youthful BUT series took their last bow five weeks later on 27 July.

A family holiday abroad prevented me witnessing the last rites being performed but, from all accounts, one understands there was little ceremony to mark the end of almost 30 years of service by the trolleys. Along with Hastings, Brighton and Bournemouth, Portsmouth was one of four select South Coast resorts to go over to silent traction, being last but one of this group to abandon trolleys in favour of motor buses. The new Leyland Atlanteans looked very smart in their crimson and white livery with full destination layouts and traditional lining. Of course, they were noisy by comparison not only with the trolleys they replaced but also with existing front-engined buses, a trend that has become more apparent with the passing of time. As I look now at photographs taken of them when new, it is strange to reflect upon their own disappearance from City streets at the time of writing. While there is no doubt they were a big step forward in 1963, carrying 76 instead of just 52 passengers seated on the trolleys, it is interesting to recall that it was possible to travel from the outskirts of the City right through to the sea front without passing a single traffic-light – if one went the right way! In some respects

subsequent developments may be seen to have been retrogade in their effect. . . . A pleasant memory I shall always associate with Portsmouth's trolleys – the only such system within the whole Solent area – is of alighting from a south-bound vehicle at Hilsea and being allowed to pull the 'frog' for service 4 to diverge for Northern Parade, Alexandra Park, Twyford Avenue, Commercial Road, Guildhall, Bradford Junction and Eastney. On pulling the handle down, a tell-tale light would come on to advise the driver that his road was set. Occasionally things would go wrong: a conductor might forget to pull the frog or it might be just one of those days, for then the poles would come off and the trolley would be stuck like a fish out of water. With all the Craven-bodied AECs and postwar buses it was possible to manoeuvre them on batteries when necessary, to avoid congestion or to reposition the poles on to the overhead using a bamboo rod carried under the platform. Even so, such antics could sometimes result in damage to the trolley-head or the wiring in extreme cases, requiring a visit from either TW1 or TW2 (the pair of tower wagons adapted from early diesel buses 17 and 18 – RV 3411/2). Long after they had assisted in the task of dismantling the overhead, both tower wagons lingered about at Eastney or North End in shabby state, forlorn relics of the last years of Portsmouth's electric phase. By a stroke of good fortune, due in no small part to the policies of a long-serving Chief Engineer (Mr Melbourne) who understood the simple virtues of Leyland engineering in the 1930s, both former buses and their contemporary Crossley Condor cousin (ex-74, RV 720) have survived to be preserved. To make their retention all the more plausible, AEC trolley No 201 has been recalled from Beaulieu to be transformed to its prewar eminence at Eastney. Whilst the casual visitor to the City might never know of Portsmouth's past connections with electric traction, at least both an early tramcar and the first trolley bus have been saved for posterity by an enlightened Corporation.

25
Summer Saturday

One of the pleasures of the summer holidays from school was to be able to see (and hear!) the vast number of extra passenger trains that were woven into an already-busy timetable. There was a carefree feeling, a certain joie-de-vivre that encouraged early rising, an air of expectancy at what the day might bring in the way of unusual motive-power or out-of-course running – in short, the special atmosphere of a still predominantly-steam railway stretched to the limit to carry holidaymakers to their destinations. The Southern boasted, in its Rail-Rover brochures, of services from Kent to Cornwall– on occasions like these one was tempted to believe it, for through trains and extra trains appeared all over the system with wondrous dexterity. Let us roll back the frontiers of time for a little to recall some of those Solent summers. . . .

It is true that most people remember the nicer things in life and happy memories are often bathed in sunshine. But even summer Saturdays were not always fine! One busy weekend in the 1950s was marred by a steady downpour with intermittent cloudbursts, yet the trains still ran and the holidaymakers – their ardour somewhat dampened – continued to travel to their distant destinations in Sussex, South Wales, the West Country or just across the Solent to the Garden Isle of Wight. For a Southern enthusiast no summer was complete without at least one Saturday spent at South-ampton Central. On the wet day just described it was necessary to shelter under the huge platform awnings, avoiding the occasional drip that always aimed for the back of one's neck, with little chance to use a camera to advantage. If it wasn't driving rain blowing on the gleaming lens it would be steam whipped-up in the wind to obscure a limited frontal shot near the platform's edge. Hurrying passengers burdened with luggage were not sympathetic to a young photographer's pleas not to cross in front of his camera in such weather conditions – one might just as well leave the thing at home in these circumstances and merely enjoy watching the trains. Surrounded by the nasal tones of the station announcer, the procession was truly magnificent: 'Merchant Navy', 'West Country' or 'Battle of Britain' Pacifics losing their feet on the heaviest loads, with splendid pyrotechnics to match, or the steady, reliable power of unflappable 'King Arthur' or similar mixed-traffic 4-6-0s taking out 10-coach trains like the Poole-Newcastle. Then, as on every day throughout the year, it would be time for the announcer's *pièce de resistance*: 'The train approaching Platform 4 is the 12.30pm all-Pullman Car train for Bournemouth, calling at Bournemouth Central and Bournemouth West only. Supplementary tickets are required for this train. Southampton Central, Southampton Central! Change here for Southampton

Docks and Cowes, Isle of Wight. Southampton Central'. The 'Bournemouth Belle', resplendent with its Pullman chocolate and cream carriages – some more than 30 years old – was guaranteed to attract attention any time, but on a summer Saturday the platform would be thronged with dozens of spotters taking numbers, eager to admire the big green engine, desperate for a drink of water from the column near that vast gantry of semaphore signals. As the Southern had no water troughs, important junctions like Salisbury or Southampton Central provided an excellent opportunity for crews to replenish supplies during inevitable delays while loading and unloading dozens of passengers with their luggage. While a train for the Bournemouth line occupied Platform 4, it was not unusual for others to be queuing block behind block to St Denys for, at Southampton, Salisbury to Portsmouth services linked with main line connections bound for London or the Dorset coast. Into this complex it was necessary to find room for the occasional train to Birkenhead, Barnstaple or Brighton as well as local services to Romsey, Fullerton, Beaulieu Road or Bitterne. Signalmen had no rest till the rush was over after tea.

But it didn't always rain. More often than not it was bright and fine, when clean engines glinted in the sunlight and carriages of all types and colours would drift in and

out as though in a slow-motion sequence. The mid-1950s remind us of the N15x 'Remembrance' rebuilds of Brighton Baltic tanks and the graceful Marsh Atlantics, of 'Lord Nelson' 4-6-0s with their unique exhaust-beat and choleric old 4-4-0s coping with 300 ton loads they dare not fail on, of former Great Western intruders coming in from Cheltenham or an unrebuilt 'West Country' passing through non-stop with a Waterloo-Swanage service. And always in the background, like a continuo for some oratorio, the announcer's intoning of train informaton. . . . 'Crossing the footbridge to Platform 2 for the Portsmouth and Brighton line. Remain on this platform for Bournemouth and Weymouth. Change here for Southampton Docks and Cowes, Isle of Wight. Southampton Central, Southampton Central. . . .'

But if Southampton captured the glamour and romance of an important mainline junction, other stations had their moments of glory, too. An hour spent at Winchester City could be most pleasant on a fine day, with a procession of trains hustling through the two-track bottleneck and a fussy little B4 0-4-0T shunting the yards to provide activity in the meantime. It was the sharply-curving sidings of Winchester City's west yard that justified retention of a pair of Adams four-coupled tanks into the 1960s, so that the passing traveller might catch a glimpse of Nos 30096 or 30102 as his Pacific-hauled express galloped by at 60 or 70mph. Three miles to the south, at Shawford Junction, the signalman would have to juggle carefully to avoid holding up a series of trains on the main when traffic was in prospect on the branch to Newbury and Didcot. As with the other ex-GWR branch running down from Cheltenham and Swindon, the Didcot Newbury & Southampton line had been shorn of most of its useful trains by 1959 as a prelude to closure, so disturbance of Saturday extras became more limited than hitherto. It was still interesting to watch the tablet being dropped or picked-up in true Great Western fashion by a Collett 2251 class 0-6-0 or a Churchward-designed 'Mogul'. But mention of Swindon-built machines reminds me that these were also evident on the main line in some numbers at the height of the season in July and August, for several additional trains were scheduled to run not only from the Midlands to Bournemouth but also south-eastwards from Eastleigh through Botley to Fareham and Portsmouth. It was not easy to predict which of these turns from or to Wolverhampton (Low Level), Birmingham Moor Street or Snow Hill might be Western-worked – it all seemed to depend on the state of affairs further north at Didcot or Oxford, where an engine-change might be effected. When a Swindon taper-boiler design was used, it might be a 4900 'Hall' or 'Modified Hall' or occasionally a 6800 'Grange'. Once, by some administrative oversight, a 'Castle' was rostered, only to be impounded by the Southern Authorities at Fratton! Apparently some platform clearances were likely to be rather too tight with those large outside cylinders. . . .

But at the risk of being considered biased, I still found it hard to beat Fareham's five-star junction on a summer Saturday. Even after withdrawal of passenger facilities from both Gosport and Meon Valley lines in the 1950s, some goods con-

Below: Typical of DN&S line trains in latter days, 2251 0–6–0 No 2240 accelerates away from Winchester (Chesil) with a down service comprising Hawksworth and Collett stock to Eastleigh./*Author*

tinued to run and the single line through Funtley Tunnel saw occasional passenger trains which still served Knowle Halt. Nothing special could be expected much before nine o'clock in the morning but, in the Southern's summer timetable for 1959, there were two departures from Portsmouth Harbour in quick succession that were both steam-hauled. First came a through train to Cardiff General, normally a Standard 4 job, followed by the initial peak-season working to Wolverhampton (Low Level) that stopped at Cosham and then ran to Basingstoke before making another scheduled halt! This might well be a task for a brass-bonneted machine, but it was difficult to photograph because of the early sunlight – failing a 'Hall' or 'Grange', a Standard 4 or 5 4-6-0 could be on the front. Within half an hour there was another Cardiff turn, often U-powered, with three DEMU turns sandwiched in while the going was good. Then expectations would run high to see what was heading the 9.40am Brighton-Bournemouth West: would it be a 'Schools' 4-4-0, displaced from the Kent Coast, or a real Brighton joke in the shape of a 4MT 2-6-4T? The first time I saw this train worked by a Standard tank I thought I must be imagining things, but no! Following the traditions of I3s and other LBSCR cross-country tanks, the 80xxx-series did quite well on this exacting turn – which was rostered for a Bulleid Light Pacific. The Bournemouth West train was another non-stop duty, with the engine restrained round the sharp curve towards Fareham station from the east, before being given its head to accelerate through the platform to about 40 as a prelude to tackling the 1 in 112 curving westward again towards Southampton. Bulleid Pacifics often slipped their wheels

Below: Complete with Western reporting number (900), No 6831 *Bearley Grange* prepares to restart the 8.50am Portsmouth-Birmingham (Snow Hill) from Fareham's platform 3 on 3 August 1957./*Author*

Bottom: Last of the Standard 4MT 2–6–4Ts to be built at Brighton, No 80154 was given charge of the 9.40am Brighton-Bournemouth through train on 3 August 1957. It makes a spirited start from Southampton Central with the heavy load, beneath a fine gantry of semaphore signals that survived electrification ten years later. /*Author*

Right: Although both L and L1 4–4–0s from the Eastern Section had been tried on Hampshire local trains in 1952, it was not until five years later that the former class was seen again. No 31777 (L) allocated to Brighton brings in the 9.40am to Bournemouth West at Southampton Central's platform 4 in 1957./*Author*

Below: Last working Atlantic locomotive in Britain, No 32424 *Beachy Head* canters down from Portchester towards Fareham with the 9.40am Brighton-Bournemouth West in fine style on 12 October 1957./*Author*

when the regulator was opened and sparks would fly skywards as the engine responded with a roar. Scorched timbers beneath the footbridge told their own tale, but it was an experience not to be missed! As an out-and-out sentimentalist, I preferred the four-coupled machines to anything else on this turn: there was a brief spell when ex-SECR L class engines Nos 31776/7 were allocated to Brighton for this purpose, following withdrawal of a number of H2 Atlantics, but they did not give of their best over this road and were replaced by three-cylinder U1 2-6-0s having more reserve. But for sheer magic it was hard to beat the old Atlantics, with No 32424 *Beachy Head* being the last to perform. I shall never forget it one autumn day in 1957, chirruping along in fine style, bucking and rocking as the crew let it take its final bow – the last 'working' 4-4-2 engine in the Kingdom. How could one ever forget, when some months earlier it had been 'wound-up' to such good effect on a westbound journey that it had overshot the platform at New Milton, requiring setting-back to let the passengers get off! Something of its char-isma survives on an Argo EP recording (made by Peter Handford), struggling for adhesion on the climb out of Brockenhurst one winter's morning. . . .

Hard on the heels of the Brighton-Bournemouth came yet another Cardiff train from Portsmouth, frequently entrusted to the Standard 4MT batch of 4-6-0s numbered 75070-75079. These had high-sided tenders of extra capacity for inter-regional duties, although all Southern engines came off at Salisbury in the normal course of events when working from Portsmouth or Brighton. Another flurry of multiple-units on local workings would be fitted in before a Brighton-Cardiff turn, which would gain a quartet of Portsmouth coaches on any other day. But on summer Saturdays the trains were run separately, with this being the first of two from Brighton. It nearly always claimed a Bulleid Pacific, usually a rebuild by the late-1950s, whereas the Portsmouth outfit merited yet another Maunsell U 2-6-0 if it was lucky. In the down direction, a little earlier, a Reading-Portsmouth train yielded an echo of the Great Western, even if it was all-stations (including Knowle Halt). Then, keeping its distance to allow a local train to be fitted into the scheme of things – dividing at Fareham for Eastleigh and Andover Junction or Southampton Terminus respectively, to economise on paths – the next Brighton-Cardiff service would roll in, loaded to 10 or 11 well-filled coaches behind another Pacific. Only 12 minutes behind that, Portsmouth's Saturdays-only through train to Ilfracombe would appear. Eastleigh might have to dig deep to find enough 4-6-2s to go round to provide one for this service; if in doubt there was always another 'Mogul' waiting in Fratton sub-shed, hopefully. Last of the pre-lunchtime through services was the Brighton-Plymouth, booked away at 12.49pm complete with restaurant car. As with the previous Cardiff duty, on any other weekday (winter and summer) through coaches from Portsmouth would be attached at Fareham, but this time-consuming ritual was dispensed with in deference to the pressures of a summer Saturday timetable. With a brief chance of water, the Pacific would top-up while passengers and luggage were squeezed into every available corner. In the restaurant car the crew were saved the hazards of serving soup while Portsmouth portions were being propelled on to the rear, though they often had a lively start when the green flag fluttered and the footplate staff decided to try and beat the clock over the non-stop roller-coaster route to Southampton. Comparative peace reigned for a while as local trains crept in and out. Meanwhile, in the down direction, no less than three inter-Regional trains had swept through without stopping, from Wolverhampton (Low Level), Birmingham Moor Street and Snow Hill respectively. At least one, possibly two, would be hauled by a named engine of GWR-origin, perhaps even sporting proper reporting numbers on the smokebox, while the third might be the preserve of that dwindling band of assorted N15 4-6-0s, the 'King Arthur' class. By this time the original Urie series had all gone, but those that remained carried with them a special interest unmistakably Southern. On workings such as these there was no chance to hear their deep-throated bark or watch their vast bogie-tenders being replenished at the water-column, yet they were an indispensable part of summer Saturdays. Finally, if one skipped lunch or brought sandwiches, there was the reward of two consecutive up trains passing through non-stop from Portsmouth Harbour to Moor Street and Snow Hill respectively. These were best observed from the bridge above the cutting about a mile north-west of Fareham on the double-track line avoiding Funtley tunnel. Here the gradient rose at 1 in 100 and sparks often ignited lineside scrub in dry weather, for any momentum gained from charging through Fareham non-stop had evaporated into a good hard slog at this point. Probably the local residents heaved a sigh of relief when the Southern turned to diesel in the summer of 1967 but, for everybody else, it was suddenly indescribably dull.

There was a further non-stop train about mid-afternoon, when the 2.45pm Portsmouth & Southsea to Bristol (Temple Meads) went on its way. A Yeovil engine was normally rostered for this duty, which might produce a high-stepping T9 4-4-0 well into the mid-1950s. Once or twice I saw No 30721 bring its train of ex-GWR coaches round the curve to form a junction with the Gosport branch, its small capuchon above the familiar stovepipe chimney giving this engine much character – particularly when it then accelerated through the station in lively fashion before disappearing out of sight beyond the coal-yard. About 30 minutes later came a regular ex-GWR working: on normal weekdays this ran to Reading General as the return leg of the 9.10am down, but on peak Saturdays it was extended through to Wolverhampton (Low Level), starting from Portsmouth Harbour yet stopping at Fareham. Finally, there came a trio of long-distance trains departing from the Harbour within little more than an hour, all of which passed through Fareham non-stop. The first of these was another Wolverhampton train, which operated throughout the summer timetable period, departing at 3.40pm; it was closely followed at 3.57pm by the through train to Cardiff, while at 4.57pm occurred the solitary departure for Sheffield (Victoria). Its corresponding down working had come in overnight, terminating at around dawn! During the afternoon a number of cross-country trains would have called at Fareham's Platform 2 bound for either Brighton or Portsmouth, as return workings of some of the morning's departures for Cardiff, Bournemouth or the West Country. In fact, as the foregoing will have shown, hardly an hour would have passed on a peak summer Saturday without a through train to or from somewhere passing Fareham. Besides all these, local trains for Southampton, Salisbury, Eastleigh and Andover had to be kept going; equally, in the down direction, a constant supply of trains had to be provided for Portsmouth to be able to turn them round once more.

If the schedule for 1959 was rather ambitious, it also took little account of engine-failures or DEMU repairs. There were two down trains in the morning, which might normally have been expected to be provided by multiple-units, which regularly appeared behind steam. The 10.15am from Eastleigh and the 10.10am from Southampton Central ran virtually to DEMU timings but with fewer stops, providing a last chance for older or second-rank locomotives to show what they could do on a tight schedule. A mixed bag of engines appeared, but T9 'Greyhound' 4-4-0 No 30120 cornered the semifast Southampton-Portsmouth train on a number of occasions while an evening return duty once produced Brighton K 2-6-0 No 32349! It was certainly rare – practically unknown – for a K to use the Netley line over the notorious Hamble bridge at Bursledon, least of all on a passenger train, though their use on the 10.03am goods from Eastleigh to Fratton became commonplace during the late 1950s and early 1960s until their demise.

Add to all the above a select group of special additional workings and the day was full indeed. A particularly interesting activity was the weekday empty stock train, which ran in the up direction with a heterogeneous collection of fitted vehicles from surplus 'loose' coaches to newspaper vans of all kinds. It might number up to 20 vehicles and was generally the preserve of something hefty, such as a 4-6-0 ('King Arthur', H15, S15 or 'Lord Nelson') or a Bulleid Pacific, because it was routed over the double-track Eastleigh line with its gradient of 1 in 100 up. Even on summer Saturdays this train used to run, passing Fareham at almost exactly 11.30am, while on a dry day its progress might be charted by the number of lineside fires started by its superhuman efforts to avoid delays. Though use of a Class V 4-4-0 on this duty might be discouraged, a 'Schools' did appear once on a running-in turn after attention at Eastleigh Works and it also provided perhaps the only chance to

Top left: Coasting because of an adverse signal ahead, K 2–6–0 No 32337 approaches Fareham with the 10.03am Eastleigh-Fratton goods, Funtley Tunnel now behind it on 15 March 1958. /*Author*

Centre left: Appropriately named for its rare visit to the Fareham area, 'Lord Nelson' 4–6–0 No 30862 *Lord Collingwood* hustles a rather lightweight ECS train up the single line to Funtley Tunnel on 7 June 1962./*Author*

Below: Complications were caused if Salisbury's turntable was inoperative. On one such occasion 2–6–0s – both Southern and Western – were required to work throughout on trains between Cardiff or Bristol and the South coast. Canton Mogul No 6338 makes a rare appearance over the Netley line with the 9.33am Portsmouth-Cardiff on 26 March 1960. /*Author*

observe a 'Nelson' at Fareham. The other complication would come from a late strawberry crop: as Swanwick yard was the main railhead in South Hampshire, a steady stream of vans for this kind of perishable traffic would run through Fareham from May onwards. In the event of a 'blackthorn winter', the strawberry crop might run on into July and no delay in shifting it would be sympathetically received by the growers, even if it meant some dislocation to carefully-planned schedules for peak Saturdays. One is left with the amusing thought that a van-load of strawberries from Swanwick might cause a ripple of delays that could be felt as far away as Sheffield or Sherborne. . . .

26
Hayling Sunset

After its usual share of early disputes between landowners and entrepreneurs anxious to proffer the unspoiled qualities of sandy beaches to an eager Victorian public, the Hayling Railway opened for business in July 1867. This 4½-mile branch curved away sharply south-eastward from its junction with both LSWR and LBSCR main lines at Havant, to meander down to Langston across the timber viaduct to the island, which was served by a tiny halt at North Hayling and a substantial terminus at South Hayling. Although operated by the Brighton line since a few years after opening, the railway remained nominally independent until the 1923 Grouping, when it was absorbed into the Southern Railway. Few changes were apparent: the name of the terminus had been altered to Hayling Island in 1892, but once the advent of Stroudley's 'Terrier' tanks had taken place around the same time, these remained in charge of all traffic despite either grouping or nationalisation. Whereas some four-wheeled coaches had been used in earlier days, these gave way to typical pre-grouping bogie stock of various types that continued to appear until well into British Railways' ownership. Electrification of the main line at Havant in 1937 led to an increase in traffic during the summer, though winter trains seldom carried more than a handful of passengers. Because its lifestyle changed so little from the late-Victorian period, I have refrained from making more than passing reference to it until now to avoid repetition.

Although the Hayling branch was single throughout its length, a second bay was available at its southern terminus. This factor, plus the run-round loops provided at either end of the line, served to encourage Southern Region management at Waterloo to take a gamble on its summer traffic potential at weekends from 1957 onwards. Whereas the normal weekday service consisted of 14 each way, with all but the first down train booked to call at both intermediate stopping-places, on Saturdays the number was dramatically increased to 24 with a half-hourly headway of alternate non-stop services between 10am and 6pm. A similar arrangement applied to Sundays for most of the day and, as the train had priority over road traffic at the key level-crossing at Langston, railway patrons were afforded an efficient, rapid service avoiding all the traffic jams that bedevilled road journeys on and off the Island. Early memories of long queues of cars, sweltering in the sun while waiting to pay their tolls at the rickety old bridge, persist from childhood; alternatively, if one resorted to the bus, it might take two hours to get aboard a single-decker either at Beachlands or at Havant! Once the new bridge was brought into use in 1956 Southdown was able to increase capacity by employing normal double-

Above: Sunday rush-hour at Havant. A1x 0–6–0T No 32640 prepares to depart with the 10.05am to Hayling Island while two more 'Terriers' (Nos 32646 and 32650) wait for the 4-COR 'Nelson' sets to clear the main line on 22 July 1962./*Author*

deckers for the complete journey, but the single road from Havant to Langston and Northney Corner was still unable to cope with the vast numbers of additional vehicles that might descend upon it on a fine day in summer. And always as the train was due, Langston's level-crossing gates would close across the road: with a cheeky whistle, one of the octogenarian 0-6-0T locomotives would hustle through – perhaps non-stop– to complete its journey in 10 minutes flat! It must have been very galling for hundreds of motorists, but the little engines could pull four coaches conveying upwards of 350 passengers each trip – maybe 700-800 people every hour – with the prospect of a pleasant walk under the trees down to the beach when the terminus was reached. Southdown was not slow to see its advantages and ran an open-deck bus past the station at a convenient moment, as well as hourly journeys by 147 from Southsea right through to Hayling – but it was only second-best. Adverts depicting the advantages of rail travel were particularly apt between Havant and Hayling!

If the ordinary weekday service, provided all the year round, required only a single locomotive, the intensive summer weekends needed three. It had long been the form to send Hayling's engine out from Fratton shed each day, rather than have a sub-depot on the Island as originally envisaged; at the end of its duties, it simply ran

back light down the main line once more. Out-of-season passengers could be catered for quite adequately by one or two carriages, which would remain in the bay at Havant overnight, while an extra coach was generally to be found in the spare platform at Hayling for use as required. Once the quayside line at Langston fell into disuse after World War II, such freight as there might be for Hayling Island was conveyed by the first train down – which omitted to stop at North Hayling Halt – operating as a 'mixed'. Likewise, for bringing back such wagons, the 2.53pm from the terminus to Havant was designated as available for a mixed train when required. On such occasions it ran into the electrified down main platform at Havant instead of its own special bay, whereupon its goods wagons would be removed by the locomotive shunting in the yard – normally a Q1 0-6-0 or N 2-6-0 tender engine. On summer weekends no such provision was made and all activity was centred upon the passenger traffic. After the usual light engine had been despatched from Fratton in the normal way, two further engines were attached to three or four carriages – which would comprise the second branch train – to double-head it along the main line through Bedhampton to Havant. They might have to wait their turn to cross over on to the branch, after which they would shunt back into the bay while the original train-set was away down the line. The pilot engine would be taken off to retire to the loop, leaving its fellow in charge of the second train. In due course this would depart for Hayling, once the first had run-round and shunted into the spare bay at the branch terminus. On arrival of the second train in the normal platform at Hayling Island, the first train would be signalled out back to Havant. Whilst it was in transit, the second train would be run-round and shunted into the spare bay in anticipation of the arrival of the next departure from Havant at the main platform. When the first train reached Havant its engine would be replaced by the spare locomotive in the loop, to allow the first engine time for coaling and watering as necessary before replacing the next arrival from Hayling . . . and so on, ad infinitum. At the end of the day two engines would return to Fratton with the spare set, leaving the third locomotive to finish the last few journeys on its own – as if it had been a weekday – before running light back to its shed in the usual way. This kind of arrangement is used by certain preserved branch lines today, when they have an intensive service at bank holiday times or other special occasions.

As time went by it seemed incredible that the Hayling branch managed to continue with its antique locomotives, although displaced main line stock had replaced the pre-Grouping carriages during 1958. The available stud of Brighton 'Terriers' had been augmented by three returned from the Isle of Wight in 1949 and their duties further east were whittled away first by the closure of the Kent & East Sussex light railway and then displacement at both Newhaven and Shoreham Docks. An exchange with one of the Lancing Works shunters yielded an engine in better condition, but it was still

little short of miraculous that such elderly machines could ensure the intensity of a summer service on the Hayling branch. The regular performers comprised Nos 32640 and 32646 – both having seen service on the Isle of Wight – with No 32650 (ex-Lancing), 32655, 32661, 32662, 32677 and 32678 (off the K&ESR) all taking their turn from time to time. Other A1x engines to appear after Nationalisation were Nos 32644 and 32659, while the last surviving A1 'Terrier', 680s, also arrived at Fratton in its final years before being exported to America restored as 'Waddon'. When Nos 32661 and 32677 were withdrawn for scrap, their places were taken by the oldest surviving engines on British Railways at that time, Nos 32636 and 32670. Both had been built in 1872 and had interesting careers. For a brief period in 1959 an ex-Chatham P class tank was tried both on passenger duties to Hayling and on shunting at Winchester City sidings, but this experiment did not appear successful and was not repeated. I have a hazy memory of an engine appearing in brilliant malachite green livery about 1950 – doubtless one of the ex-Isle of Wight examples soon after shipment back to the mainland – but otherwise the normal paintwork was lined black. Due to their long lives and varied careers, detail differences marked out each of them as being in some way unique: two had LSWR chimneys, the refugees from Vectis had extended bunkers while all exuded 'atmosphere' as well as a healthy supply of steam! William Stroudley would have been very proud of them.

At the end of the 1962 summer season, it was announced that the branch would be closed to all traffic. There was quite an outcry, with the usual objections and letters to the local press. Despite its excellent summer traffic and uninterrupted access, both locomotives and timber viaduct were getting no younger – taken overall, receipts were insufficient to cover major capital expenditure of the kind needed to fund such basic aspects of the line. Throughout the bitter winter of 1962/3, trains continued to run amid snow-covered scenes and in the sum-

Right: All Change for Siberia! A1x 0–6–0T No 32661 shuffles past a deserted North Hayling Halt in wintry conditions on 8 January 1963./*Author*

Below: Rumbling across the timber viaduct with a four-coach train, 'Terrier' No 32677 passes the fixed distant for Langston on 18 May 1959./*Author*

mer a half-hourly service operated at weekends as in previous years. But there was an air of desperation about it, now. Semaphore signals protecting the viaduct – permanently pulled off to show line clear, regardless of the direction of travel – were taken down. Defaced notices about closure were still in evidence and no one seemed to want to put his hand in his pocket to pay for a new bridge, let alone any new locomotives! The pathetic little saga was slowly played out, while a few brave souls founded a Society to try and buy the line to operate it with lightweight trams. When the summer season ended, it was just a matter of putting a brave face on things until the moment of closure – what else was there to do?

It was announced that the last public trains would run on Saturday, 2 November 1963. Business was brisk all day long, with No 32650 working the earlier trains and No 32662 appearing later to lend a hand. Finally, for the last official service, six coaches were employed, with a 'Terrier' at each end. This was done both to spread the weight on the old viaduct and to save time running-round with such a long train at Hayling. The journey was delayed by crowds of people at Havant, but at last it

147

Above: Langston station was rarely host to more than one engine at a time, for double-heading was taboo to spread the load over the viaduct. The 2.53pm from Hayling proved to be an exception on 30 July 1961, when A1x 0–6–0Ts Nos 32640 and 32646 headed the train coupled chimney to chimney./*Author*

was allowed to begin. The corridors were crammed to capacity and some of the carriages did not appear to be lit, but nobody minded. Unlike any previous 'last journeys' I had made, this one was also the very last public train. The outward stage was quite noisy, with some rousing songs and much gaiety; as if by common assent, this gradually died away until departure from Hayling was graphically solemn. With windows wide open to catch the sounds of two venerable engines on their last active duties for Southern Region, their combined exhausts were oddly reminiscent of *Lion* in the famous film about the Titfield Thunderbolt. It must have been running about two hours late, but time meant nothing. As the train approached the ghostly viaduct, moonlight cast magical shadows on dark waters below to highlight the drama of this occasion. A mournful whistle announced the approach

to Langston crossing, both engines eased for a moment before their final all-out effort against an adverse gradient to their ultimate destination. Like a phantom amid drifting smoke and steam, the two tiny 'Terriers' opened up and wound slowly along the cutting under the one and only roadbridge, the hollow puffing from their long funnels sounding most eerie in the darkness. As if controlled by one man, each wailed a shrill lament as the final curve brought them round into Havant station. Blinking in the sudden glare of bright lights, with much blowing of noses and use of handkerchiefs, this historic train gave up its passengers. A main line electric had been specially held to connect, although it was not far off midnight, but all dispersed with a heavy heart at the loss of a good old friend.

Next day was brilliant weather for the time of year, as November over the marshes is often misty and damp. It was to be in no sense an action-replay of the previous day, for this special last train was to be a fleeting visit by Society members from London and the Home Counties – an ideal excuse for an orgy of photography but nothing more. By dint of some brisk driving, I managed to see the excursion emerge from Funtley Tunnel

Above: No longer frustrated at Langston crossing, Southdown Leyland Titan PD2/1 381 (JCD 81) was providing a relief service between Hayling and Havant one summer's day in 1966 – already the undergrowth had begun to take over following closure of the railway. No 381 itself was withdrawn shortly after, having spent most of its career in the Portsmouth area./*Author*

hauled by one of the original Urie S15 4-6-0s, No 30512, before the specially-prepared engines for use on the branch reached Havant. From an overbridge near Bedhampton I watched them bring a five-coach load of modern high-capacity BR suburban stock up from Fratton – the two tiny engines glinting in the winter sun and quite dwarfed by their coaches. It was interesting to see two A1x engines double-heading, since this was never seen on the branch itself, apart from summer weekend shunting of an additional train-set within station limits at Havant, referred to earlier. But did I say NEVER? As in politics, so in transport, never is a long time! In fact, on one occasion I did catch Nos 32640 and 32646 in tandem at Langston, chimney to chimney, with the 2.53pm from Hayling – in addition to the rare fact of them double-heading at all, No 32646 was also facing towards Havant instead of the more usual method of working chimney-first to Hayling. However, although this final excursion ran empty from Fratton with the engines in harness, on arrival at Havant the leading locomotive (32670) was detached and moved to the rear of the train, repeating the previous night's exploit with

their stock sandwiched between them. By this means the special would have a locomotive chimney-first in both directions, something much appreciated by the myriads of photographers who descended upon the area that fateful Sunday. Of the journey itself I cannot speak – being a lineside observer – but with perfect weather and an imaginative day's programme, the spectacle must have made a fitting conclusion to 96 years of operation. Anyone who saw No 32636 heading the train to Hayling, while No 32670 enjoyed that distinction on the return trip, could not fail to have been impressed with the turnout of BRs two oldest active locomotives, 91-years old apiece! Both have since found an honoured place on preserved railways – what a pity the same cannot be said for the 'Terriers' Railway', the branch to Hayling Island.

27
The Price of Independence

We have seen in earlier chapters how the welter of small independent operators provided grist to many takeovers throughout the inter-war years, but some at least managed to keep going while others stepped into the shoes of those who wished to retire from the scene without handing over to a major company. World War II provided a breathing space, since many large operators had to yield some of their best coaches as part of the needs of the Ministry of Defence for the Services. As peace returned there were a few hectic years when the small operator had a field-day, but when deliveries of new buses and coaches were resumed in earnest in 1948/9 the superior resources of major public service fleets began to tighten competition to breaking-point. While Messrs Blake and Prince had sold out to Provincial in 1939, providing it with services to Alverstoke and Stokes Bay, it took another 10 years to take over most of the other independents in Gosport. All were local routes, such as Hathaway and Hutfield who both operated to Grange Crescent, while the 'Premier' fleet of Main ran between the Ferry and Chantry Road. G. A. Cross' 'Perseverance Motors' had a service to Brockhurst, but this together with the others mentioned above came under the control of the Gosport & Fareham Omnibus Company by the commencement of 1950. It was another three years or so before Dyer's two services were taken over and Provincial

Green held sway in Gosport, concluding a battle for supremacy that had been going on since the days of grandfather's trams!

With the southern flank secure at last, some thought could be spared for the position in the Fareham area. The Fareham Market-Catisfield Post Office service had been the preserve of E. A. Millard then Glider & Blue until 1948, when it was absorbed by Hants & Sussex Motor Services. One could not fail to be impressed by its modern lowbridge Leyland double-deckers displaying service 14 blinds – but their reign was comparatively short-lived, being replaced by AEC and Guy double-deckers (highbridge, of course!) from Hoeford at the beginning of 1955. Weeks later, the Funtley-based buses of F. C. J. Smith's Fareham-Knowle service gave up and another route (18) was added to Gosport & Fareham's tally. At first it had to be operated with aged AEC Regals of 1934 but, as both service 17 (to Catisfield) and 18 to Knowle Hospital ran past the home of Mr H. Orme White, it was to be expected that changes would come sooner rather than later. I have already mentioned that rebodied double-deckers fresh from a sojourn at Readings' coachworks were to be found on the Catisfield route, while Sunday visits to the Hospital prompted use of a double-decker during the afternoon, for a while. A less-publicised use of a double-decker, albeit open-top, was on the last

journey each evening during summer from Fareham to Knowle before returning to Hoeford Depot. The bus completed its day's tour of duty after a spell on service 10 to and from Stokes Bay, which was a more likely stamping-ground for an open-air machine, but providing the weather stayed fine night-duty nurses and refugees from Fareham's hostelries were happy to use it! Twenty years before the coming of the M27 Motorway past Funtley, the raucous sound of a Gardner-engined Guy Arab ascending their 1 in 10 at 11pm must have been less than popular with local residents. My last week's duty as a conductor with Provincial during the summer of 1955 was spent on this late-return, covering Stokes Bay and Knowle with utility Guys 18 and 56 alternately. No ordinary return fares were issued on the Stokes Bay service, but day returns were available from Fareham Market to Funtley (8d) and Knowle (11d), for which Bell-Punch tickets were required as TIM's were not all equipped with such a facility.

Above: Three cream bands and the nice old shade of tramway green made Provincial's few open-toppers look very smart. Utility Guy No 18 (EOR 876) with Park Royal bodywork waits for custom at Stokes Bay (Alverbank) during the summer of 1963./*Author*

Right: Regal re-bodied. Following the time-honoured principle of 'make do and mend', the 1934-vintage Harrington-bodied AECs were progressively up-dated with a full-front design by Readings. No 30 (CG 9609) was first to see the light of day in its new guise on 18 May 1957 in Fareham's West Street./*Author*

Even so, single 1d adult fares were still being issued on most Provincial routes, though the newly-acquired services from Fareham referred to above had a minimum fare of 1½d on some stages and 2d on others.

Soon fares had to rise, but as a consolation Provincial commenced a policy of face-lifting some of their oldest buses – notably the conversion to one-man operation with full-fronted bodywork by Readings of the surviving AEC Regal antiques. No 30 was the first to be thus modernised, entering service once more in June 1957. Yet within days had occurred the dreadful fire at Hoeford, which posed a major threat to the Company's continued existence. However, with goodwill and practical help from Southdown in providing a couple of prewar Leyland TD4/TD5 double-deckers for a few months, the Company was able to purchase some surplus AEC Regents from a number of sources as well as an ex-Midland Red utility Guy. The rehabilitation programme for older vehicles was stepped-up and some chassis were salvaged from the fire to be reconditioned and rebodied by Readings. We have already seen that some of the wartime Guys had been rebodied, too; this process continued with full-fronted designs becoming the norm after the creation of a second 'coach-bus' number 60 in 1956. A pair of new Guy Arab Mk IV double-deckers entered service in this guise in 1958 while, later the same year, came the first 'conversions' to be equipped with the revolutionary Deutz air-cooled diesel engine. Almost unique in Britain in this respect, Provincial pursued the Readings-bodied Guy-Deutz theme to make it their hallmark in the 1960s, with no less than a dozen hybrids plus one highly-experimental AEC-Ruston. The last-mentioned cannot be considered to have been an unqualified success and reverted to conventional power with an AEC 7.7 litre unit in its final years, having taken over the fleet number 14 from an equally unusual vehicle created during the war – once an AEC Mandator tanker lorry! Perhaps Mr Orme White's patronage

of the Deutz air-cooled engine may be traced to his father's German ancestry, but Hoeford became the happy hunting-ground for a number of scrapped Guy chassis purchased from dealers, in addition to those converted from buses already in the Company's ownership. One or two had part of their full-fronted bodywork constructed at Hoeford, being sent to Hilsea for their final treatment by Readings, but the rest were built there in their entirety. Later 'conversions' or reconstructions were required to be re-registered as the official view was that these hybrids were, in effect, new vehicles. Possibly the most unusual and bizarre of all the Deutz machines was the last, built in 1967 when Mr Orme White was well over 80 years of age. It was the solitary single-deck example and was specially constructed to work over the tortuous railway bridge at Knowle to help out the ailing AEC Regals,

Below: Last of the line, No 8 (HOR 676E) was the only example of a single-deck Guy-Deutz. The massive air-cleaner ('Dalek') can be seen above the near-side window, illustrating why all these hybrids had full-fronted bodies. It spent most of its short life on the Knowle service./*Author*

by then incredibly elderly. It was a noisy beast, with perimeter seating and licensed to carry standees, but it represented the ultimate creation of a genius, whose like public transport may never see again. If its five years' reign on the Knowle service is not mourned by those who used it, this bus must surely have been one of the most curious vehicles ever to have passed through the maw of the National Bus Company!

But if air-cooled diesels were stealing the limelight at Gosport & Fareham, the reader should not assume that this trait was its exclusive metier. Always a ready purchaser of promising second-hand vehicles since between the wars, Hoeford became home to a whole generation of former Southampton Corporation Guy Arab buses and six more from Red & White Motor Services – the only lowbridge buses ever owned by Provincial. Those from Southampton brought the hiss of air-brakes to Brockhurst and Bridgemary, while the lowbridge vehicles took over the Foster Wheeler contract for construction workers at the Fawley Refinery, in previous years the preserve of some interesting prewar AECs, including a couple formerly with Glasgow Corporation having the endearing registration BUS! But whereas all Gosport & Fareham Guys bought new had been equipped with Gardner's quaint five-cylinder engine, including some Mark IV models as late as 1958, the secondhand invasion between 1963 and 1967 was dominated by the more powerful 6LW version. While the newcomers from South Wales were nearly always used on contract duties, usefully fitted with heaters and platform doors, the FCR-registered group that had grown old beside the Itchen came to spend their declining years on flatter terrain adjoining Portsmouth Harbour, where open platforms and a lack of heating might pass unnoticed among residents used to the primitive comforts of Deutz power!

But while the ranks of the aged Regals were being reduced by the inexorable passage of time, the days of double-deck sup-

Below: The 'new look' in a strange place. Seddon No 45 waits at a temporary stop in Paxton Road, Fareham, while working an unusual circuitous route avoiding the A27 railway arch under Fareham station, when this was being reconstructed on 23 March 1969./*Author*

remacy were soon to be challenged by a new generation of single-deck buses as unusual in their way as the first three-axle Chevrolets had been in ousting the trams 40 years before. In 1968 and again the following year, two series of Seddons appeared in a smart new livery with much larger areas of cream paintwork. The first batch consisted of nine bodied by Strachans with six Pennine examples delivered in 1969, both series having dual doorways and licensed to carry 15 standee passengers in addition to 40 seated. Their new livery made the double-deck fleet look distinctly shabby, a situation that was soon remedied by an experimental repaint of number 70, one of the two Guy Arab Mark IV vehicles purchased new in 1958 – only a small number of double-deckers ever aspired to this variation, which was achieved by using a brighter green, and enlarging the amount of cream around lower-deck windows in addition to the complete roof and upper-deck window area. A more significant change was the style of fleet name, hitherto a fancy script, and the abandonment of Provincial's traditional garter at the rear: within a further six months the complete establishment had been sold to the recently-formed National Bus Company, an amalgam of the nationalised British Transport Commission fleets with those formerly controlled by their major rival, British Electric Traction. After 31 December 1969 the Provincial Traction Co Ltd came to an end.

Whilst overall control passed to the NBC in the shape of Hants & Dorset at Bournemouth, including legal lettering on the vehicles being changed from Hoeford to The Square, yet Gosport & Fareham Omnibus Company still survives being a statutory creation, ensuring the fleet's nominal independence even within the state-controlled umbrella. It will require another Act of Parliament to abolish that! Although further secondhand vehicles were acquired in some numbers – seven Bristol LS6Gs with Eastern Coachworks bodies of various types and a lightweight SUL4A bus for

Knowle services as well as seven double-deck AEC Regent Vs from City of Oxford – yet the old pioneering Provincial spirit was not quite extinguished, although it was to be frustrated and its last offspring stillborn. Shortly before Hoeford relinquished its grip on its own affairs, it had ordered a batch of six new Daimler Fleetline rear-engined double-deck buses with Roe bodies – an imaginative choice that would have looked marvellous in the Company's own livery – but it was not to be. Despite the arrival of ex-City of Oxford double-deckers, it was decreed that the Gosport & Fareham fleet should become the NBCs first all single-deck outfit; the Daimlers

Above: Destined to achieve 36 years' service with Gosport & Fareham Omnibus Company, AEC Regent No 34 was still on 'main road' duties (service 3 to Gosport Ferry via Anns Hill) on 6 January 1969, passing under the doomed railway arch at Fareham station. */Author*

Left: Under the monarch's eye, King Alfred Motor Services' lowbridge all-Leyland PD2 LAA 822 represents the vanishing independent at the end of the 1960s./*Author*

Below: Garter, white diamond and scroll. A last look at the old Provincial image on 30 March 1969. Relics of the tram days were still visible all around at Hoeford. /*Author*

were switched with six new Bristol RELL dual-doorway saloons from Hants & Dorset and never made it to the banks of the Hoe, though a couple were used at Southampton for a while before joining their banished sisters at Poole. For many the dying gasp of the old Company was epitomised by its three survivors from the 'good old days', Nos 24, 27 and 34. The first two were Regal saloons (rebodied by Readings during the early 1960s) while the other was the oldest double-decker purchased brand-new in 1936 – this trio of AECs lingered into 1970, when 27 had the distinction of actually dying on the job as its timing-chain snapped whilst on service. The other Regal was sold to a scout troop and gallant old 34 went to the scrapyard at Fort Wallington, where many other local buses had met their end, to be gutted and burned on a funeral pyre.

Another long-established firm in the Winchester area was also to sell out to Hants & Dorset in 1973. King Alfred Motor Services, controlled by the Chisnell family, will be long remembered for its image of the monarch on either flank of its buses, as well as for generations of Albions, Leylands and AECs. But if many old-established names have gone, some have managed to survive and outlive the steam age: Eassons, Glider, Coliseum and Summerbee (now Princess Summerbee) are still in business, the first two mentioned having limited stage-carriage services too. Southern Motorways sprang from the ashes of Hants & Sussex, keeping alive many of the old routes. Even Aldershot & District has become Alder Valley, while Wilts & Dorset slowly faded away in the grip of its southern neighbour. Liss & District lingered into the 1970s but is now just a memory. In Portsmouth some famous names have gone, like Triumph, Don and Royal Blue Coaches (no relation to the coach fleet of Southern and Western National, of which the former name has since vanished) though Byngs and White Heather may still be seen. Hutfield's coaches and a handful of secondhand double-deckers for schools and private-hire work no longer survive in Gosport, but Priory Coaches keep alive independent tradition by the Hardway, For the vast majority, sadly, the price of independence has been just too high.

28
The Years before BTC + BET = NBC

So far as Hants & Dorset Motor Services Ltd was concerned, this chapter might almost have been entitled 'Between Renumberings' since such a major exercise occurred both in 1950 and again in 1971. However, the latter is outside the scope of this present volume and I shall confine myself to the situation as it existed up to 1969 – the fateful year of nation-wide amalgamation by former British Transport Commission companies (the Tilling Group) with their private-sector counterparts owned by British Electric Traction to create the National Bus Company.

If the fleet lost something of its special 'character' when the old class letters were abolished, the new numbering system instituted on 1 January 1950 by Hants & Dorset had the virtue of being logical. Perhaps to avoid possible confusion by duplication with Wilts & Dorset, numbers commenced at 500; blocks were allotted to different categories of vehicle, although in some cases these had to be extended when the original blocks were exhausted. Broadly the position became that service stock was numbered up to 549 and then from 2000 upwards, while small-capacity single-deck buses (consisting of a handful of Dennis Ace and Bedford saloons) occupied the block between 550 and 599. Coaches began at 600 and continued from 850 to 899, while single-deck buses were allocated 700-849. Double-deckers commenced at 900 and

eventually reached 1577, but as older vehicles were withdrawn at the lower end of the series their numbers were gradually allotted to new coaches, continuing from 899. The adoption of a policy of one-man operated single-deckers led to expansion of their numbers at the expense of double-deckers, with a fresh series appearing at 3001 to cater for this. In fact no new double-deckers were added to the fleet after purchase of its final FLF Bristol Lodekka in 1967, a policy that caused numerous problems in the early 1970s when fashion switched back in favour of one-man operated high-capacity buses for urban duties.

Looking back over the postwar years, the overall impression of Hants & Dorset's policy is one of conservatism. However, in the early 1950s, there was a break with traditional designs when large purchases were made of the new underfloor-engined Bristol LS model for saloons and coaches and the equally-novel Bristol LD Lodekka, all with Eastern Coachworks bodywork. While other companies and municipal fleets were investing in conventional Leyland PD2 designs and a variety of half-cab crew-operated single-deckers, Hants & Dorset's dual-doorway LS5G buses were something of a surprise – the practice of entering these buses at the rear and alighting through the front was not long continued, being replaced by normal front entrance OMO with the rear door being panelled over. A number of these saloons could be seen showing signs of their twin-entrance origins after almost 20 years in service, while NRU 9 (796) even retained its coach seats – although its fellow 'DP' NRU 8 (795) had them replaced by the normal leatherette variety but with a reversing window let-in to the rear panel. Of the Lodekkas, Hants & Dorset acquired pre-production model 003 (LRU 67: 1337) which featured on Bristol publicity literature of 1953 and was subsequently demonstrated to several other bus fleets in the South. Its unique radiator grille made this bus instantly recognisable throughout its long association with H&D, though it spent much of its life at Bournemouth.

While displaying commendable courage in choosing avant-garde models in preference to the tried and tested K and L series still chosen by Wilts & Dorset, Thames Valley and others, another novelty appeared in the shape of a pair of Beadle/Morris Commercial saloons intended for use on the rural service 66 (Salisbury-Whiteparish-Romsey-Hursley-Winchester). Because of their design, it was not considered practical to adapt them for OMO, so 777 and 778 (JRU 62/3) survived as crew-operated single-deckers in the Lymington area until 1962. But several of the Bristol L-type single-deckers were converted, those from 30ft long LL saloons being rebuilt with hideous full-fronts that did absolutely nothing for their image! Conversions of former coaches were not always so drastic, but demotion from the predominantly-cream coach livery to green rather took the shine off them. Eighteen out of 24 Portsmouth Aviation-bodied coaches were lengthened to 30ft and rebodied with Eastern Coachworks full-fronted saloon design for bus work, after 10 or 11 years in original guise. With such a large batch, the rebuilding was phased over a period of two years from 1960-1962. The four 1949-built vehicles (663-666, JRU 66-69) retained 7.7 litre AEC units, while 670 and 671 (KEL 65/6) were re-engined with Gardner 5LW 7.0 litre engines. All the remainder were provided with Bristol AVW 8.1 litre power-units in place of their original 6LW kind, which were used instead in some of the Lodekkas. Quite a few rebodied buses had cut-away rears for possible use on the Sandbanks-Shell Bay Ferry section of service 7 –

Below: Two representative examples of Hants & Dorset's fleet from the 1950s: Bristol LS5G saloon 789 (MLJ 141) was one of the first horizontal underfloor-engined vehicles to be operated, while 1368 is typical of many Bristol LD and FS double-deckers purchased since 1953. West Marlands (Southampton) bus station appears deserted on a Sunday morning!/*Author*

Right: The highbridge Bristol KSWs of Hants & Dorset were the last of a long line of K-types dating back to 1938. No 1334 (LRU 63) squeezes under Fareham's railway arch on a local journey from Heathfield Estate (service 73) on 6 January 1969./*Author*

a regular feature of travel between Bournemouth and Swanage, but a number of them ended their days on Lee-on-the-Solent or Hill Head duties from Fareham. Even after their services were no longer required with H&D, these survivors of traditional front-engined design were sold off to schools or scout groups, while a handful were re-painted in Wilts & Dorset red livery and transferred to Andover or Basingstoke for further use! Incidentally, 677 (KEL 405) once appeared in a film entitled *West Eleven* shot around Corfe Castle; after a period of semi-retirement as Scouts transport at Godalming, it has been finally preserved. When living at Alton in February 1973 I came across one of the red-painted examples on an evening trip back to Basingstoke – its licence expired and looking very scruffy – quite possibly the last active survivor of a long line of Bristol L-types that had begun with BOW 162 in 1938.

But if single-deckers were exceptionally long-lasting with Hants & Dorset, traditional Bristol K-types were not far behind. At Eastleigh, Woolston and Fareham depots a modest number of lowbridge K, KS and KSW models kept the flag flying on schools, works specials and relief journeys until the end of the 1960s, with some vehicles achieving a score of years in service. Their simplicity of design and ease of maintenance, in addition to a certain popularity among the crews, helped to prolong their activity at a time when no new double-deckers were being purchased. Apart from the loss of the upper cream band (below the upper-deck windows) and some painting-out of destination apertures, there were few changes in appearance or character since the first deliveries of postwar Bristol Ks started to arrive with ECW bodies. The 60-seat highbridge examples (1299-1336) were the biggest single departure from

usual practice, but a large proportion of these went to Poole anyway. Like all crew-operated, open platform buses they look old-fashioned now. . . .

Aside from the simple principle of front-mounted vertical engines being retained, Southdown had given a more-modern style to its fleet with the introduction of Northern Counties forward entrance design of 69-seat double-deckers purchased between 1957 and 1967. Despite some simplification of livery and curtailment of destination information, achieved by abandonment of indicators over the platforms and reduction of the rear display to route number only, the Southdown bus and coach fleet at the end of the period covered by this book was still recognisable as upholding virtues entrenched by half a century of public service. In a word it was developing in its own mould – unique but excellent. If years of association with Harringtons, the coachbuilders at Hove, came to an enforced end after their classic Cavalier and Grenadier designs in 1962, further attractive coaches appeared for use on extended tours in subsequent years bodied by firms whose styles were universal but which gained something from Southdown's livery. Leyland Leopard chassis became the new 'standard' in succession to generations of Tigers, Royal Tigers and Tiger Cubs with a natural extension into the range of single-deck buses. On the lighter

158

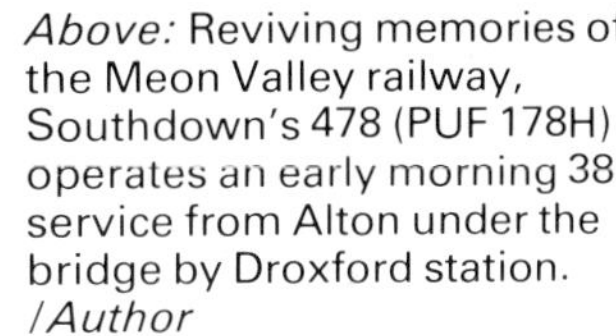

Above: Reviving memories of the Meon Valley railway, Southdown's 478 (PUF 178H) operates an early morning 38 service from Alton under the bridge by Droxford station. /*Author*

Left: Municipal liveries have been less prone to sudden change. The City of Southampton was still operating Guy Arab buses on normal service in full traditional livery, like 229 (HTR 46) on route 15A from Swaythling along Burgess Road on 8 May 1969. /*Author*

Below left: Docks Tours were very popular in the 1960s, with both 164 and 167 providing farewell glimpses of the great Atlantic liners. The former paused for photography beside the Dry Dock during a visit on 14 September 1969./*Author*

159

side prewar Cubs and Cheetahs had given way to three varieties of Commer coaches, while a new bodybuilder appeared to help equip the Leopard buses – Marshall of Cambridge – along with groups by Weymann and Willowbrook. Perhaps in anticipation of what was to come nationally, Southdown had taken delivery of 60 Bristol RE rear-engined buses by the end of the decade, all bodied by Marshall, split into both short (RESL) and long (RELL) varieties to suit different requirements. The last display of Southdown's special flair for individuality, before NBC corporate policy needed to be considered, came with a series of 30 dual-purpose single-deckers in 1968/9. Among the tallest vehicles of their kind in the country – their height is 11ft 6in – Northern Counties designed the 49-seat bodies for these Leyland Leopards, numbered 450-479 in the fleet. They were somewhat controversial machines in various ways, although undoubtedly following tradition set by prewar Tiger 1400s and postwar 1500-series Royal Tigers. Perhaps I may allude to one aspect which excited comment on their arrival by saying that, in my personal opinion, this design is one of the few that has actually gained from current NBC paintwork modes – they were delivered in light green with dark green band below the windows. Portsmouth obtained a handful, using them on Southdown's rural 38 route through to Alton – an extension of the old Droxford service, after closure of the Meon Valley railway in 1955. It was my privilege to travel upon two Leopards at different times between Alton and Wickham on this route, an experience I much preferred to journeys made with Bristol RE vehicles. Perhaps it's just that I don't have much sympathy with the principle of rear-mounted engines!

The position has changed out of all recognition in the 10 years following formation of the National Bus Company, for who would have imagined that Southdown, Hants & Dorset (including the now-defunct Wilts & Dorset), Aldershot & District (now Alder Valley) and Provincial would all be joined in one conglomerate? More striking, and disappointing, for the man in the street is the loss of long-established local associations by the expunging of all individual fleet liveries, to be replaced by a depressing three-way 'choice' of National white, green or red. Even if many fleet-names remain in use, their style of presentation is now so completely uniform as to be meaningless and almost an insult to the proud names and traditions built up over half a century and more.

Below: Rebuilding of war-damaged Kings Road was matched by rebuilding 25 postwar Crossley buses with prewar Leyland running-units from scrapped TD4s. In modified form the Crossleys proved most useful as trolley bus replacements, though this led to the abandonment of route letters for motor buses in 1963. /*The News, Portsmouth*

29
Plebeian Paddler and Sterling Steam

When one has been fortunate enough to be offered a 'lift' on the footplate of a Bulleid Pacific locomotive No 34054 *Lord Beaverbrook*, after waiting to catch a train to Portsmouth on Fareham's draughty station one cold winter's evening, the memory of a 20min thrilling ride is not likely to be erased by the passage of time! It is just one of many personal pleasures that remain, associated with the Age of Steam. It also illustrates one of the innumerable instances of kindness that I and many other railway enthusiasts received from professional railwaymen in the period of steam's eclipse. Whilst I had once been allowed to drive a tiny saddle-tank when shunting slate wagons at Port Penrhyn, Bangor, and in more recent times have been able to handle a diminutive Krauss 76cm gauge engine along the upper reaches of the Mur Valley in Austria amid unspoiled alpine scenery, yet the brief journey in pitch darkness on the vast footplate of *Lord Beaverbrook* must rank in equal value for its evidence of the sheer mastery of a big steam locomotive at work in its natural habitat. Not that I am in any way belittling the efforts of preservation societies and other organisations in providing steam tours or regular services on branch lines up and down the country; rather that the circumstances are now so different.

One by one, the Southern's relatively small stud of steam locomotives was being reduced as diesels took over more of their work or – under the Beeching plan – services were rationalised (a euphemism for being discontinued), so making them redundant. It seemed as if, for every one engine scrapped, two dozen railway enthusiasts would emerge from hiding and appear to haunt every closure, every 'last train'. The cult of gricers was born to plague staff with interminable questions and comments, demanding 'souvenirs' in the shape of anything from tickets to totems. Sad to say, a minority disgraced themselves and all genuine enthusiasts by resorting to pilfering, with the result that the last years of steam witnessed some of the scruffiest-looking locomotives – bereft of name- and number-plates – ever to have wheezed and clanked their sorry way to the scrapyard. Trespassing was rife and called down the management's severe displeasure on all and sundry, including those with official lineside photographic passes, whose privileges were then curtailed to the detriment of all. It was a time of little joy: the railway's image tarnished by Beeching's dogma and enthusiasts looked upon collectively as a scourge upon society, making it difficult for the old 'understanding' to survive. One – no, two – good things came out of this period, for the more responsible enthusiasts rose to the challenge and achieved aims previously deemed impossible or impracticable in saving certain portions of branch or secondary line for future restoration to traffic in private ownership. Funds for the purchase of engines, rolling-stock and even several miles of track were increasingly successful to enrich our railway heritage in years to come for the benefit of all. The second good portent was the firm establishment of the 'Special Train' as a feature of future railway marketing policy for railfans. Although this has usefully widened into coverage of all forms of traction – diesels have become 'respectable' in the 1970s – the undercurrent of pressure for live steam on main lines built up during the iniquitous years of complete embargo until British Rail cautiously began to release its safety-valve through a 'Return to Steam' committee. Before main line steam on the Southern finally ceased, it may be timely to revue the position as it developed in the years 1962-1967.

Once it had been agreed with the Science Museum that a representative collection of locomotives and rolling-stock should be established as part of the national collection, there was some intense lobbying regarding what should be included – and what left out. In my own small way I contributed by writing letters to both Waterloo and the District Motive Power Superintendent at Eastleigh, Mr S. C. Townroe, to try and secure a Drummond T9 4-4-0. Fortune and the Railway authorities smiled upon these efforts for a LSWR 'Greyhound' was, indeed, selected and in the end the choice lighted upon a local engine, No 30120. Although it spent a short period helping out on the far-flung North Cornwall line, of the survivors it was found to be in the best all-round condition and was restored to working order during the winter of 1961 for occasional use on special duties.

Below: Creme de la creme! Even hard-bitten railwaymen stopped for a second glance at 120, when it appeared in Eastleigh shed on 9 March 1962 after overhaul and restoration to running order./*Author*

Externally, it was given a chimney capuchon and painted in LSWR green – an attractive livery, if historically inaccurate, due to the engine not having been super-heated and fitted with its extended smoke-box and stovepipe chimney until Southern Railway days – before re-appearing as No 120 in March 1962. Other fine engines had been restored externally for display in the combined Transport Museum at Clapham, including original Stroudley A1 0-6-0T *Boxhill*, Adams T3 4-4-0 No 563 and a South Eastern & Chatham D class 4-4-0 No 737. Also earmarked for preservation were examples of 'Schools', 'Lord Nelson', 'King Arthur' and 'Battle of Britain' classes of passenger locomotive. But of secondary and goods classes it was possible to put aside only a couple of tank engines and the wartime 'Austerity' Q1 0-6-0 No C1. At least, with uncertainty at an end, it was possible for private groups and individuals to make offers to save particular favourites and the measure of their success can be seen on preserved railways throughout England, with proportionate rewards in the Isle of Wight with items of an especially parochial nature following the end of steam traction there on 31 December 1966.

It was inevitable, but still surprising, that requests should be made by organisers of steam tours for locomotives from other parts of the country to be allowed to oper-ate on special charter trains. The precedent had been set by Mr Alan Pegler with his *Flying Scotsman* locomotive following its purchase in 1963 and subsequent use on BR's main lines, although Capt W. G. Smith had achieved this result with his pre-served Great Northern saddle-tank in 1962 on a Victoria-Sheffield Park Bluebell Special. But the internationally-famous A3 Pacific was given licence to travel exten-sively over 'foreign' lines on BR that had never been considered possible by most enthusiasts – despite its vast size, it was permitted to visit Fareham and adjoining areas in 1966! Other unlikely machines appeared on the Southern, including more former LNER Pacifics of Classes A2 and

A4 as well as privately-preserved 3-cylinder 2-6-0 No 3442 *The Great Marquess* – a long way from its native West Highland line in Scotland! While the variety was refreshing, there was a feverish haste underlying every-thing, almost as if the world was due to come to an end on 9 July 1967. . . . We know, with hindsight, that it did not: while some appeared to be totally unaware of the momentous occurrence about to take place in their midst, others quietly took pre-cautions to enable life to go on with some degree of normality even after the end of steam, while the maniac fringe wound themselves up to fever-pitch and beyond. As I viewed the bleak prospect of future weekends stretching endlessly into infinity, bereft of what seemed to be an admirable

Below: On a depressingly damp day *The Great Marquess* came to Fareham. Restored as No 3442 of the LNER, Gresley's 3-cylinder 2–6–0 glistened in the rain and reflected the soft light from Victorian gas lamps as it passed by on 12 March 1967./*Author*

Above: A short-lived combination of electric and steam power was provided for the Brighton-Plymouth through train for a few months in 1964. Bulleid C-C electric loco No 20003 approaches Nutbourne with the 11.30am from Brighton in January 1964./*Author*

relaxation and simple pleasure, it appeared sensible to put 9 July firmly into perspective in the middle of a fortnight's holiday abroad where the authorities appreciated the true value of steam! Before vanishing into the mountains of Europe, I felt it right to take my leave of the Southern in fitting manner with a Pacific heading the 'Bournemouth Belle' westward out of Southampton Central. On Thursday, 8 June, I promised myself one last ride on this famous all-Pullman train before it vanished for ever along with all steam motive-power when the Waterloo-Southampton-Bournemouth service was officially electrified the following month.

Blessed with sunny weather, I took a day's leave from selling motor cars to frustrated railway travellers and drove to Southampton Central – I still called it that, although the Terminus station had closed in September 1966 – to buy half-day returns and Pullman supplementary tickets to Bournemouth Central. As the tickets were purchased for Ingrid (my German girl-friend) and myself, I was reminded that Bournemouth West, the old terminus of the 'Belle', had closed in 1965. Once on Plat-

form 4 things looked quite promising, for rebuilt 'Merchant Navy' 4-6-2 No 35007 (formerly graced with the name *Aberdeen Commonwealth*) was in the adjoining bay, simmering with that self-satisfied smirk that all Bulleid Pacifics seemed to have. With familiar tones the station announcer's voice came over the amplifier, as if calling the faithful to prayer. But the throbbing roar of our approaching train was not an admired steamer but one of the borrowed Brush Type 4 diesel locomotives, called in by Southern management as a stop-gap measure to alleviate difficulties experienced in trying to maintain increasingly decrepit coal-fired machinery. But if the motive-power may not have been to my liking, the passenger accommodation certainly was. The non-stop journey was pleasantly swift but one was able to enjoy both the view and the quality of one's surroundings without disturbance. At Bournemouth, the day was saved by No 35003 *Royal Mail* appearing to work a stopping train to Weymouth and we climbed aboard to savour what proved to be our final steam-hauled journey on any Southern main line.

On the last day of June I got up at the crack of dawn to take a look at the Longmoor Military Railway, where steam was also due to be reduced to the ranks of the seldom employed. It was a beautiful morning, clean and fresh after a heavy dew over-

Left: Efficient? Yes. Aesthetic? Well....
No D1708 in two-tone green livery throbs
purposefully away from Lyndhurst Road
station with the down 'Bournemouth Belle'
on 9 April 1967. /*Author*

Below: As the handful of passengers
climb aboard the one-coach train, Army
saddle-tank No 195 eases forward to run
round, in preparation for the next
departure from Liss (LMR) to Longmoor
Downs on 30 June 1967. /*Author*

Bottom: Steam's final hour (1): Last steam
push-pull train in Britain, or at least on the
Southern, the Lymington branch was the
M7s refuge until 1964. No 30480 bustles
along with a two- coach set in December
sunshine.
/*Author*

night. As I reached Longmoor, a plume of
steam could be seen rising above the roofs
of the cluster of brick buildings beside the
road from Liphook. Stopping my Riley
Kestrel to investigate, I was just in time to
see 0-6-0ST No 195 come off shed to take a
single carriage down to Liss to meet the first
electric train from Portsmouth. With
proper military precision, the guard
switched on the flashing lights to warn possible road traffic of the incidence of a train at
one of several ungated level-crossings,
while signals at such an early hour were
honoured more in breach than in obser-
vance. Hastening away towards Liss Forest,
I hoped to photograph the little train in
truly rural surroundings before the sun rose
high in the clear blue sky – so blue that it
nearly matched the Army livery adopted
for all its railway rolling-stock since my
leaving school. Perhaps the driver knew I
was trying to take a picture of his train, or
maybe he was in no hurry, for I reached Liss
Forest in time to capture an idyllic scene.
With a hoot entirely in keeping with its
colour-scheme and reminiscent of Caledonian locomotives in Scotland, 195 puffed
lazily across the road, white steam lingering
in the still air amid the trees. Finding a nice
spot in a field close to the embankment, I
waited for it to return from the junction,
bringing some of the civilian personnel
employed at Longmoor's Royal Engineers

establishment. While waiting, I pondered on the little pleasures that could come the way of a railway photographer: total peace in lovely surroundings, the sun on one's back while bees and butterflies savoured freshly-opened flowers. . . . Of course, it was never like that all the time (I had many a wet shirt to prove it), but as the last days and hours of steam in the south ticked away one was aware – acutely aware– that it was not just an era that was drawing inexorably to a close, but a whole way of life. My reverie was interrupted by a cheerful toot from 195, bustling back from Liss with lots of white smoke and a healthy chestful of steam. Passengers waved, the shutter clicked and it was time to think of breakfast – and my dew dampened trousers!

The following day was a Saturday. After a hectic round of preparations for foreign parts. it dawned on me that I had totally neglected railways for at least 24 hours. In order to expiate such a sin of omission, I ventured out to see what might be in charge of the 2.02pm through train from Ports-mouth Harbour to Sheffield (Midland). At steam's final hour such a train, running once weekly in either direction, might be a candidate for something tucked in the back of Eastleigh's murky shed – a Standard 4 or 5 4-6-0, even a Pacific perhaps? Having borrowed a tape-recorder to immortalise the sound, I waited in anticipation beside the double tracks of the deviation under Highlands Road bridge. Five years before there had been a landslip in the damp cutting and one track was now out of use, rusty and overgrown, it being considered uneconomic to repair such secondary routes. This had meant that all northbound traffic, with the exception of a handful of very heavy

Below: Steam's final hour (2): For just a couple of weeks in August 1963, 9F 2–10–0 engines based on the Somerset & Dorset line for weekend passenger duties found weekday employment from Salisbury on the 11.27am Chichester goods. No 92206 brings loaded coal wagons under Northern Road bridge into Cosham during this period – sadly, the practice abruptly ceased. /Author

trains forced to use the single-line through Funtley Tunnel, came up the 1 in 100 gradient 'wrong line' out of Fareham, while all down trains without exception came through the tunnel – a situation that presented some local difficulties with single-line tablets between Knowle Junction and Fareham East box! A supply for Knowle had to be collected by motor cycle from time to time. Through the archway of the bridge one had a clear view of proceedings, but the throbbing vibration of terra firma that presaged the train's arrival had nothing to do with steam. Yellow-fronted 'Crompton' Type 3 No D6550 came up the hill with characteristic panache before curving away out of sight. The brief reign of Standard 9F 2-10-0s on Salisbury-Chichester goods, of 4MT tanks on the 5.20pm Eastleigh-Fratton Works train and anything steamable on parcels traffic at Christmas time was over – the sands of time had just run out.

But while, for a couple more years, open days at Longmoor would bring back the welcome Caledonian hoot or raucous whistle of a steam locomotive for a brief season, like the cuckoo in spring, even the Royal Engineers' railway was doomed to closure. For a few months it provided a haven for privately-owned steam engines in need of repair or restoration, yet soon enough they would be moved on like gypsies — it seemed as if the simple delights of steam railways had been officially declared socially unacceptable! Everywhere changes were coming thick and fast: on the Portsmouth Direct line the long reign of Maunsell's 'Nelson' 4-COR and 2-BIL electric units was drawing to a close, though some survived long enough to be painted in

Below: Going . . . Diverted from Eastleigh via Botley, Fareham and Netley due to electrification work on the main line, after an engine change at Fareham No 34046 *Braunton* restarts the magnificent array of Pullmans following reversal of the 'Bournemouth Belle' on 22 November 1964. / *Author*

the new-image blue livery, while a steady trickle of goods yards were ceasing to be open for business, in favour of major concentration depots maybe miles from the customer. A last pleasure was permitted for one more season in the Solent, when ordinary passengers and lovers of the steam age could relish a voyage on board PS *Ryde* between Portsmouth Harbour, Clarence Pier and Ryde, Isle of Wight. Last of the Solent paddle-steamers to be built, just before the war in 1939, *Ryde* had done her bit at Dunkirk and been demobbed in 1945 to give years of pleasure and faithful service on regular sailings to the island. In later years first the huge *Whippingham* and then the smaller *Sandown* were withdrawn and sent to the breakers – was this fate to befall the last in a proud line of Southern Railway paddlers? As one stood peering into the engine-room with its spotless machinery and burnished piping, mesmerised by the effortless rise and fall of marine big-ends, the question posed itself again and again – why this wholesale destruction, what blindness was leading us towards the 'plastic' society, why, why? Orderly progress was one thing; the monumental folly of indescriminate abandonment of valuable assets was nothing short of an aberration of the first magnitude. Was this the day of Armageddon? The white-heat of anger and resentment at this seeming conspiracy to destroy passed and I saw again the steady pulsing of the pistons, while every even revolution wiped the moving parts with oil to maintain the whole wonderful contraption in perfect working order. This was logical, practical – a haven of common sense in a world increasingly dominated by the whim of fashion or short-term financial considerations. The steady progress of 'You've never had it so good' Super-Mac had swollen the bubble of success to an impossible size and soon it must burst. For us lemmings it was downhill all the way. . . .

Below: Coming . . . Framed in the arch of Highlands Road bridge, No D6550 tackles Fareham's 1 in 100 up towards Eastleigh in earnest with the Saturdays only 2.02pm Portsmouth Harbour-Sheffield (Midland) through train on 1 July 1967./*Author*

Conclusion

30
What Goes Down Must Come Up

In his tragedy *Macbeth*, William Shakespeare coined a most memorable phrase: 'Things at their worst will cease, or else return again to what they were'. Entirely apposite to transport in Britain no less than to the Solent in particular, the message is one of hope: hope that, in the 1970s, the depressing downward spiral might be halted and sanity break out everywhere. As I write this in the summer of 1979, 10 years beyond the natural terminal reached by this book, that hope is slowly being fulfilled. Whilst the nadir was reached in 1972/3 – when NBC liveries were in a shambles, political instability loomed dangerously over the horizon and the Mid-Hants railway between Alton and Winchester closed after a long fight – salvation came from a most unlikely quarter. When war flickered briefly in the Middle East and sanctions curbed the developed nations' insatiable demand for oil, rationing of fuel was achieved by a combination of increased price plus a general shortfall in deliveries and suddenly – miraculously – the case for public transport could be seen and heard loud and clear for the first time in a generation. As the price of petrol and cars has soared in a decade to almost four times what it was, so a new sense of responsibility, realism, restraint has begun to emerge. No longer is coal derided as old-fashioned; British Railways has long since lost its sick joke music-hall image. For every new penny that North Sea oil rises in price, the case for public transport – and some switching of energy resources – grows stronger by the minute. This is not the place to prophesy on the future but, by the end of this century, it should be clear that the 1970s marked a turning-point for our roads and rails.

As we look forward in hope, secure in the knowledge that public transport has a major role to play in the future, this is perhaps the right moment to remember what has been achieved in preservation of our heritage. A couple of old Southampton tram-car bodies have been found, to be lovingly restored in the years ahead, to join knifeboard open-top car No 45 as examples of the last full-size active tramway in the Solent area. Portsmouth, as we have seen, had an enlightened approach to its transport treasures a long time ago – a recent Open Day at Eastney Depot (itself an innovation) enabled visitors to see the former horse-tram No 84, Thornycroft J open-top bus BK 2986, first AEC trolley bus 201 and Leyland Titan TD4 RV 6368 all in juxtaposition – the youngest exhibit being 44 years old! As time goes by one hopes that an example of Provincial's Portsdown & Horndean Light Railway cars might be restored, since three are known to exist in various stages of decay. Of the older buses, Southdown has restored CD 7045 – a 1922 Leyland G7 open-topper that began life as a charabanc on solid tyres – to immaculate condition to rival its still-original Titan TD1 UF 4813 of 1929, the former having been retrieved from hiding at Hoeford when Provincial joined the NBC-fold in 1970. Steam trains have returned to part of the Mid-Hants Railway. Privately preserved examples of cars, lorries, fire-engines, vans, buses and steam-engines of all kinds are too numerous to mention: when one considers that there are Rallies, Shows, Steam-ups and 'Runs' practically each weekend from April to October to cater for every taste, it is as though the whole nation has become afflicted with a harmless dose of nostalgia!

That such events have become very popular is beyond question – what was once considered in some circles to be an eccentric hobby has blossomed into a national attraction appealing to all ages. What better way to learn history than to see it re-enacted? How better to curb vandalism than by showing proper regard for man's genius and artistry in the development and design of everyday transport? Yesterday's novelty may easily become tomorrow's treasure. . .

Below: Saved! Squatting like a guru at the entrance to its old lair – Southampton Docks shed – B4 0–4–0T No 30096 has found a home on the Bluebell Railway in Sussex./*Author*

Bibliography

The following are suggested for further reading:

Periodicals (all monthly)
Buses, Modern Tramway, Railway World, Modern Railways (all Ian Allan Ltd), and *Railway Magazine* (IPC Ltd).

Historical and general publications
Allcock, G. A.; *Gosport's Railway Era*; Gosport Historic Records & Museum Society, 1975.

Bradley, D. L.; *Locomotives of the LBSCR* and *Locomotives of the LSWR*; RCTS, 1972, 1967.

Course, Edwin; *The Portsmouth Papers No 6*; Portsmouth City Council, 1969.

Course, Edwin; *The Southampton & Netley Railway*; City of Southampton, 1973.

Harman, R. G.; *The Hayling Island Railway*; Branch Line Handbooks, 1963.

Harrison, S. E.; *Tramways of Portsmouth*; LRTL, 1955.

Horne, John; *Farewell to the Floating Bridges*; Southampton City Transport & the Southampton University Industrial Archaeology Group, 1976.

Jones, B. C.; *Crossing the Itchen*; Southampton Corporation, 1960.

Klapper, Charles; *The Golden Age of Tramways*; David & Charles, 1974.

Milton, A. F. & Bern, L. T. A.; *Portsmouth City Transport 1840-1977*, 1977.

Morris, Colin; *History of the Hants & Dorset Motor Services Ltd*; David & Charles, 1973

Southdown Utility Guy Arabs, 1973; Southdown Fleet & Routes 1939-1974; Southdown Fleet & Routes 1949; 1977 (all Southdown Enthusiasts' Club).

The Southdown Story 1915-1965; Southdown Motor Services Ltd, 1965.

Hants & Dorset Motor Services Ltd, 1968/9; Gosport & Fareham Omnibus Co, 1968/9; Southdown Motor Services Ltd, 1971 (all Fleet Histories; PSV Circle & Omnibus Society).

Hampshire Telegraph & Post 150 Years Souvenir; Portsmouth & Sunderland Newspapers, 1949.

100 Years of Southampton Transport; Southampton City Transport & Southampton City Museums, 1979.

Portsmouth 75 Years of Transport; City of Portsmouth Transport Dept; 1976.

Southdown Buses & Coaches, 1950; GWR Locomotives, 1947; Southern Locomotives & Electrics, 1946; British Railways Locomotives; British Railways Diesels; British Electric Trains; Locoshed Book (all Ian Allan Ltd ABC Booklets).

Various timetables and farecharts published by local bus companies referred to in the text, Southern Railway timetables, Bradshaw's Guide and Southern Region timetables (British Railways).

The Sounds of Bygone Transport (Argo Records TR 139).

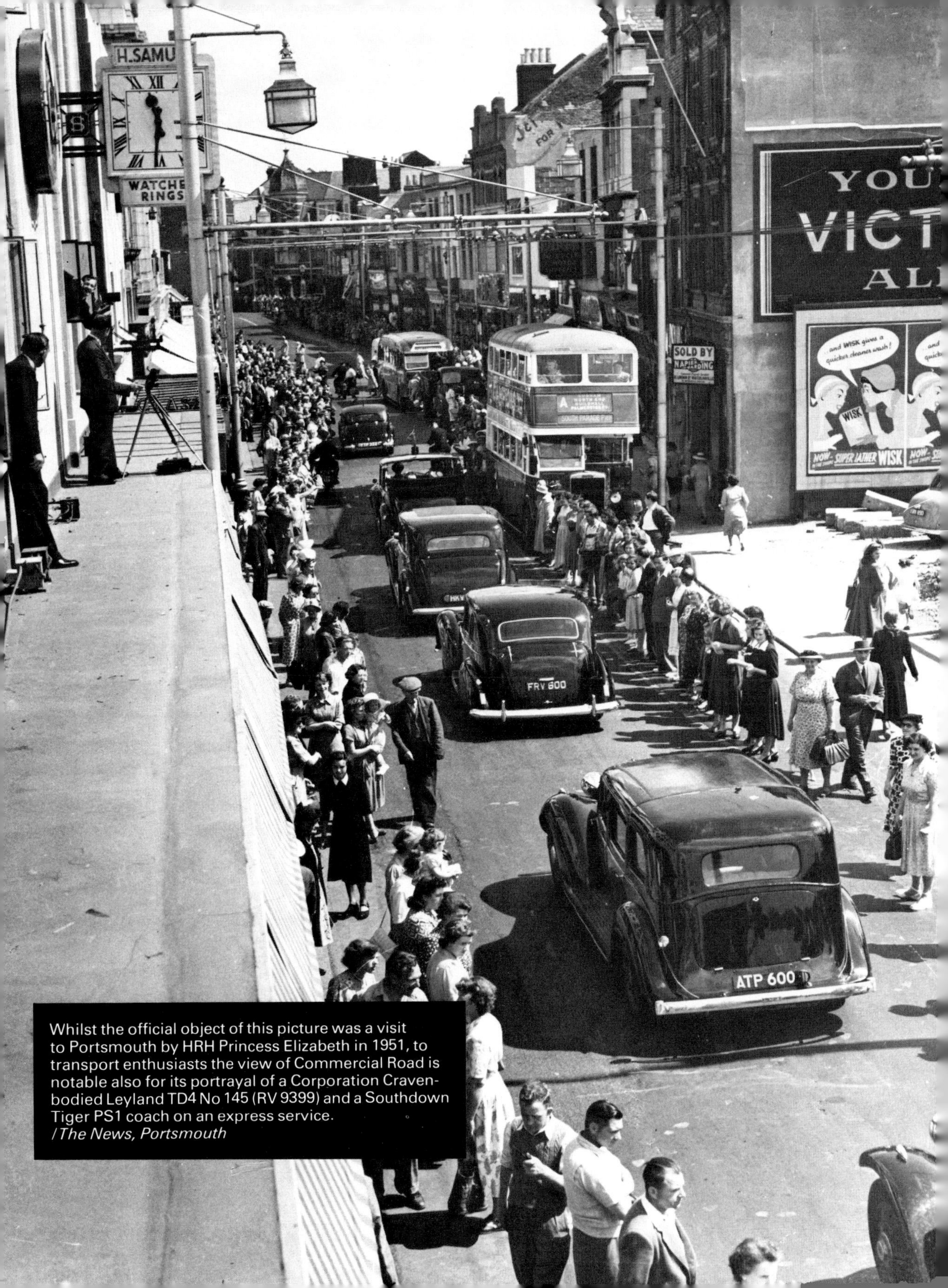

Whilst the official object of this picture was a visit to Portsmouth by HRH Princess Elizabeth in 1951, to transport enthusiasts the view of Commercial Road is notable also for its portrayal of a Corporation Craven-bodied Leyland TD4 No 145 (RV 9399) and a Southdown Tiger PS1 coach on an express service.
/The News, Portsmouth

Index

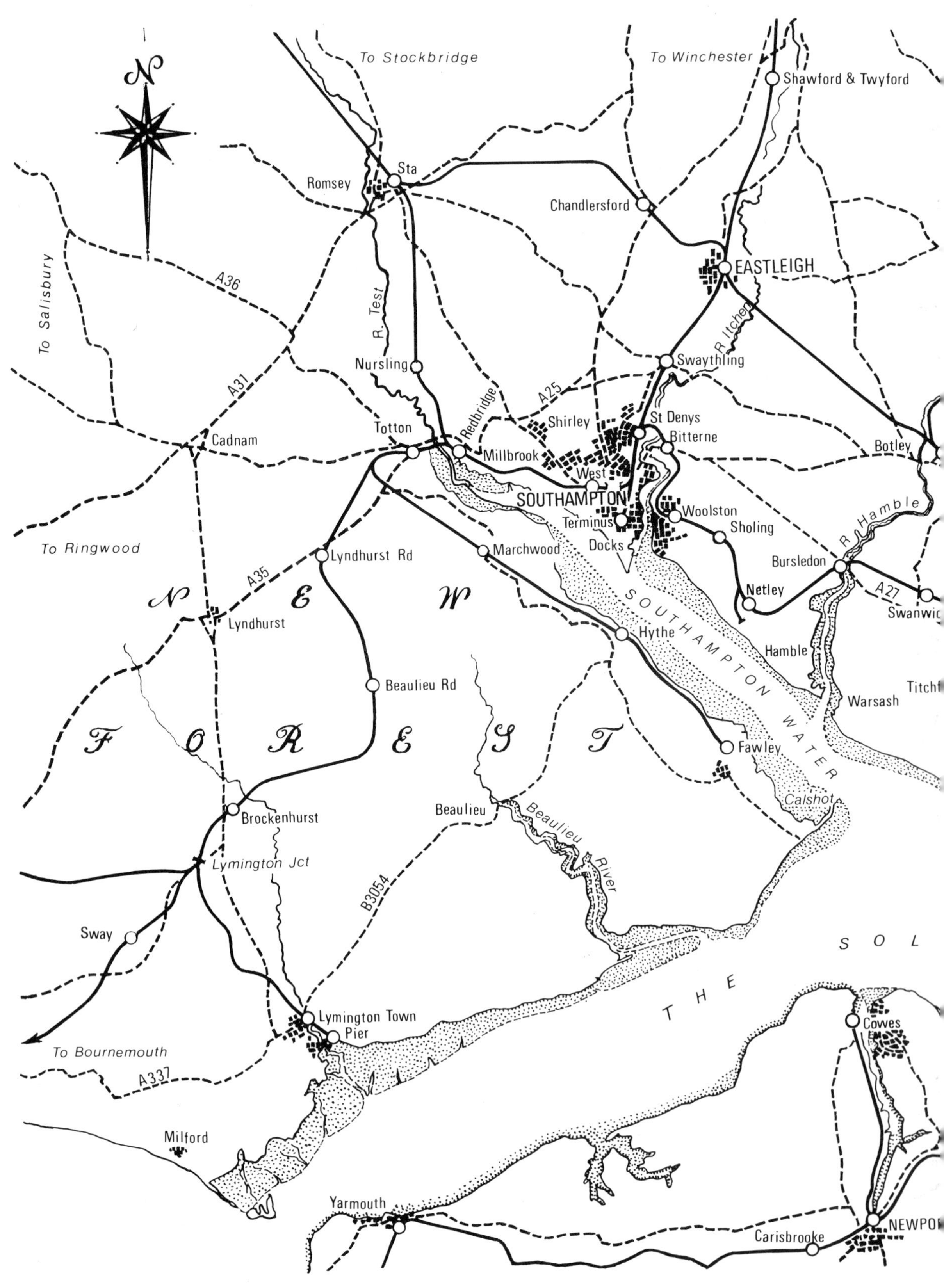

N
To Stockbridge
To Winchester
Shawford & Twyford
Romsey
Sta
Chandlersford
A36
EASTLEIGH
R. Test
R Itchen
To Salisbury
Swaythling
A31
Nursling
A25
Redbridge
Shirley
St Denys
Bitterne
Cadnam
Totton
Millbrook
Botley
West
R Hamble
SOUTHAMPTON
To Ringwood
Marchwood
Woolston
Terminus
Sholing
Docks
N
E
W
Lyndhurst Rd
A35
Bursledon
Lyndhurst
Netley
A27
Hythe
Swanwic
SOUTHAMPTON WATER
Hamble
Beaulieu Rd
Titch
Warsash
F
O
R
E
S
T
Fawley
Brockenhurst
Beaulieu
Beaulieu River
Calshot
Lymington Jct
B3054
Sway
THE
SOL
Lymington Town
Pier
Cowes
To Bournemouth
A337
THE
Milford
Yarmouth
NEWPO
Carisbrooke